Behind Closed Doors

Stories from the Inside Out

by

Students at Scriber Lake High School

Behind Closed Doors: Stories from the Inside Out

Cover photo by: Jacquie Lampignano
Cover Design: Danielle Anthony-Goodwin

Edited and compiled by Marjie Bowker and Ingrid Ricks
With Assistance from Danielle Anthony-Goodwin and Jennifer Haupt

Proofreading by Carol Bowker and Mary Anthony

Print book and ebook formatting by Hydra House
www.hydrahousebooks.com

Published by Scriber Lake High School
A program by
www.weareabsolutelynotokay.org

For privacy reasons, some names have been changed

*This book is dedicated to Captain James "Rock" Roth
who believed that students at Scriber Lake High School could soar*

TABLE OF CONTENTS

OUR INTENTION WITH
THIS STORY COLLECTION

W e have come together as writers—some facing our lives for the first time on paper—to open the doors of our souls. We have traveled back into the darkness through hospital doors, closet doors and prison doors, through doors of the heart and the mind, to remember the details of the people and events that have changed us.

Some of us write to remember and some of us write to forget. Some of us write to leave parts of our stories behind in order to find closure and peace. All of us write to show you who we are. Only from understanding the stories behind each other's scars can we really know the truth of what we hide behind.

We hope you will be encouraged to emerge from behind your own doors to find the power of forgiveness and understanding with us.

THE MONSTER WITHIN HIM

MARIKA EVENSON

The news anchor appears on the TV screen with the words "child rape arrest" and a picture of handcuffs above him. My stomach is in my throat.

"A man already convicted once of child rape is now suspected of raping another child, and KIRO7 reporter Amy Clancy has dug up the details. She's live downtown where the suspect just went before a court," he says. My hands are clammy as I rub them up and down on my tense, trembling knees.

The screen flashes to a wrinkled blonde woman. "Forty-two year old Jeffrey Evenson is a Level Three sex offender. According to these documents, he has raped again. His alleged victim—a then six-year-old girl," she says and my heart evaporates into thin air.

I see multiple mug shots of my father, and even though I'm disgusted to have the same last name as him, I'm thinking that the reporter could at least pronounce it correctly.

Then the real news begins.

"He was convicted in 1990 for child rape, in 1998 for child molestation and he was convicted twice for failing to register as a sex offender. On Tuesday, he was arrested again in Seattle for allegedly raping a now nine-year-old girl after the girl's father called police."

My ears turn off, my eyes blur and I feel a heavy pressure in my chest. I can only hear bits and pieces now. I can barely comprehend the phrases "dead mother," "pornographic movies" and "fondle her."

I can feel the vomit wanting to come out of my body, but I don't let it. I take one last look at the picture of my father and my lip trembles.

She has just unveiled my father's evil to whoever is watching the news.

"If Evenson is charged, he could be behind bars for the rest of his life."

I want to rip his DNA strands out of my body.

I try to recall the sound of his voice, but I can't. It seems like a distant memory, or maybe a whisper the wind blew my way. I remember how he looks, though, and his smell, and the way he acted the last moments we spent together at Hemp Fest just a few weeks ago.

We walked at sloth speed through the crowded event—my friends far ahead of us—as I listened to the thousand-mile-a-minute speed of his words slamming together. I could smell the whiskey on his breath. He took the last sip of it from the Dr. Pepper bottle without sharing.

"Thanks, Jeff," I laughed. "I wanted some of that."

"You're very welcome, Daughter," he answered.

He always found ways to make sure I knew he was my dad and I his daughter. We didn't always get along, but after my suicide attempt, him being in jail practically my whole life and my mom's skin cancer announcement, I wanted to be with him. I wanted to have a relationship with him and this was the first real step. I was excited and scared because every time I tried this, something would happen and it wouldn't work.

He pulled out a menthol cigarette, so I took it and sparked it. He pulled another out for himself. We walked and smoked, swerving through the crowd, looking for my friend, Stephanie. All I could smell was the menthol tobacco and weed on us, which was nothing new. My dad always smelled of this "cocktail" of alcohol, weed, and tobacco and I was starting to follow in his footsteps. I had been hurting my body for months with reckless behavior and drugs. I didn't care about my body. I just wanted to feel numb and would do anything it took to feel that way. I kept it my own dirty little secret.

He could tell that I was not okay, and when he looked at me with our deep, always-changing eyes, I couldn't even make full eye contact because all I could see was how we were each other. I have always resembled him, but unlike me, he looks like a monster from a movie. He looks like Freddy Kruger before the angry parents burn him. Unfortunately, just like Freddy, he had a perverted mind for children and raped them. The difference was that he didn't kill the kids.

We found Stephanie and then we all walked to a music tent and sat on the grass. He pulled out his O2 tank, which resembled a soy sauce bottle with a long, clear hose attached and a metal bowl piece in the center.

My friend pulled out his bong and we started smoking. The music filled my ears as I went into a daze. My body felt numb the way I liked it and I went into my own little perfect world until my dad pulled me out of it by leaning over and saying, "I'm really happy you came."

He passed the tank to me. I hit it and said, "O ... of ... course."

"No, I mean it, because I don't know how long I'll be around. There's this bullshit going around that I've been raping this kid for a while." He said this so simply, his eyes and face so innocent, like he had just told me something minor. Like what he had just told me wasn't crazy or horrible.

My heart sank instantly. I was repulsed. I thought he had changed. I thought he had changed for me. He had promised me he would. I was so angry I wanted to let out a blood-curdling scream. But I didn't. I just stared at him.

"Her mom was killed, too, and they're trying to pin it on me."

His face was unchanged by what he had just said. It seemed like he had just told me that the sky was blue or that fish lived in the water.

I looked to my friends and realized they hadn't heard him. I quickly sparked a cig. "Wait. What? Like murder? Like they think you killed her?"

"Yup," he answered.

Could my dad really be a killer? My mind was in a whirl trying to make sense of his words.

"What? Why? Did you do it?" I asked over the loud music. "How did she die?" I could feel my thoughts pressuring in my head. My eyes wanted to let the tears out but all of the weed and smoke from the hit covered it up.

"She was suffocated with a pillow in her sleep," he said. I took a hit from the bong and hit my cigarette heavy and long. I didn't ask any more questions because I didn't want to know the answers.

We stayed there and smoked and ate on the rocks by the beach until we were all high and tired and then we got up to leave. He gave me a hug but I pulled away quickly, thinking the hands trying to go around me could be the hands of a murderer. The hands that took away girls' childhoods, ruining them forever. Maybe that's why I had been molested—as karma for my dad doing it to little girls.

He said, "I love you."

I couldn't say it back.

I watched him turn and walk into the crowd that washed over him like a wave.

We got back to my house and I loaded a bowl from the eighth he had given me. My friends and I smoked some more. I didn't know how to tell them what my dad had told me in the tent. So I just came out and said it. "My dad said that he might get arrested for rape and murder."

"Do you believe him?" Stephanie asked. Her face was empty because she already knew the bad things he had done.

All Chris said was, "Damn, Homie. That's crucial. I'm so sorry. That's fucked up."

"I don't believe it," I said. "I mean he might be a bad person but I don't think he could actually murder someone."

Somewhere deep down in my clenched-up, broken heart, I knew he had done it. But I didn't want to say the words out loud.

We stayed up smoking until three in the morning and then went to bed. My mind started racing, thinking of all the worst things. I thought about the night he had called me when I was going to kill myself. I remembered how upset I was when he would vanish for months. I was thinking about murder and if he could really do it. I knew he had choked my mother before, but I never would have thought he could kill a person. *Could he really have been raping her daughter for three years?* I silently cried and fell asleep with nightmares of pillows on an unknown woman's face.

❧

Three weeks later, my mom asked the question I already knew was coming because Stephanie had warned me that she wanted to talk. "Can you come on a drive with me?"

"Sure," I answered.

We drove for a while in silence with awkwardness between us. She handed me a Newport cigarette. She never did this, so I knew whatever was wrong was pretty bad. She eventually spoke up.

"So, I wanted to talk to you about something and I didn't know the best way to tell you, so I took you for this drive so we could be alone. It's pretty bad, but I told you I would always be honest with you. Uncle Nutty called this morning. Your dad was arrested the other day in Seattle.

He was homeless. He was arrested for rape and is under investigation for murder. This is his third strike and I heard he is going to be on KIRO 7 News ... "

I started crying. I didn't want it to be true, but it was. I tried to talk, but all that came out were muffled sobs. My eyes stung. I tried to take deep breaths, but every time I did there was a stabbing pain in my left side.

"I'm so sorry, baby. This isn't your fault," she said.

I finished my Newport and sat, crying.

"Is this my fault?" I vented through my sobs. "Did he do this because of me? Why is he my dad? I wish I was dead, I wish he was dead."

We got back and pulled into the driveway. I watched the garage door go up in slow motion, then got out of the car and slammed the door behind me as if my dad was in it and I was cutting him off from me forever. My mom would usually comment on something like that, but she kept quiet. She came to my side of the car and gave me a quick hug.

Inside, I told Chris and Stephanie what I had just learned, even though I had already texted them the news. All I could do was sit on my dingy blue, burnt-spotted carpet and cry, waiting for the 5 o' clock news.

※

I stare at the TV screen but I don't really see anything.

How could he have done those things? How could *that* be related to me? Why had he broken his promise and lied?

I'm ashamed of my life for being his daughter and I don't want to be here. I don't want to be related to a monster.

I feel dead inside. Why do I miss someone so much when they were never really there in the first place? If I had been born a boy like all the doctors predicted, would I be like him or would I be different?

I turn the TV off and just sit on the carpet saying nothing. Stephanie and Chris are there. I love them but I want them to leave. I just want to be alone. I need to be alone. But I'm so upset that I can't even find the words to tell them to leave. So I light the tank and suck through the long hose, hoping it will take me away from this place and numb my mind.

I wipe my eyes as if I'm wiping him off of me. I get up and go to the bathroom and when I look in the mirror, I see him in the reflection. I bend my head, wipe my eyes again and look up to see my own puffy-eyed, red face.

I want to shut the door on all the ties to my father.
I want to open the door to a new and better life.

A Note from Marika

It's been about six months now and I haven't heard anything other than that my father is still awaiting trial. I have finally realized that I'm not my father and that I could have never changed him, no matter how hard I tried. I still have the hole in my heart from never really having a father, but I don't feel it so much anymore. I'm eighteen and now live with my fiancé and will be getting married. I stopped doing drugs about a month after hearing what happened because I don't want to end up with problems later on. I learned drugs are not the way to get over my problems, nor is alcohol. All I can do is be strong and ask for help when I need it. I still battle with cutting but I'm doing the Butterfly Project and it helps me get into the mindset that I don't need to cut anymore. After finishing high school, I plan to either become a chef or a counselor to help those who are lost or hurt. I hope my story can help those who have a parent or family member in jail and have felt the same way I described in my story. I want you to know that it does get better.

"If one door opens to another door closed,
I hope you keep on walk-in' till you find the window."
"My Wish"—Rascal Flatts

MY ROMEO

LILLY ANDERSON

As I inhale the fine lines of crushed painkiller off the dirty bench, my phone vibrates. It's my mom.

"Are you around anyone?" her text reads.

"Yes," I type, glancing up at my friends.

"Step away from everyone and call me."

My mom and I are close, she is one of my best friends, and I can tell by her request that this must be serious. My mind races and my hands start to tremble. I step away from my friends without saying a word. They're too busy passing the pipe to notice. I walk under the nearest tree to escape the hot sun and dial my mom's number as I try to get my thoughts together.

I think about the past couple days and what this phone call could be about. But scanning my memories, I can't think of how any of my craziness could get back to her. Even though she is my best friend, I keep my demons tucked away. I start to calm down as she picks up the phone. She makes me reassure her nobody is around before she tells me what she has to say.

"Romeo's dad came by today," she starts out.

"You mean his foster dad? What did he say?" I reply, thinking nothing of her words. Romeo is my boyfriend of about three months and he has been living with us for the past two months. My mom agreed to let him move in because he was a foster child and was being passed from house to house in the church system. He had also just gotten out of the hospital from months of treatment for heart cancer when we met.

"That's why I told you to call me," my mom continues. "He never had a foster dad. When his dad stopped by he showed me proof that Romeo is his real son, and that he has lied to us about everything." I can tell by the tone in her voice that she is just as stunned as I am. My palms start to sweat as I walk a little bit farther away from the group. I feel the warm sun on my back as the panic sets in. My heart pounds as I try to think of a response.

"What do you mean?" I finally ask.

I hear my mom sigh before she replies. "He was never a foster child. He was sent here from Texas to live with his dad because he beat up his mom. He only wanted to live with us because his dad doesn't allow drugs or cigarettes near the house."

I'm speechless. There is a frog stuck in my throat. I try to choke it down but it won't budge.

"He doesn't, nor did he really ever, have cancer, and his real name is Austin."

Her last sentence sends the blood rushing through my veins and my cheeks start to get warm. I glance over and see him laughing with all of our friends and a cold shiver races down my spine. They have no idea about the secrets I have just unlocked. *I've been living with and dating a complete stranger for three months now. I gave something I can never get back to someone who couldn't even tell me his real name.*

"What do I do?" I ask, trying my hardest to hide the panic and desperation in my voice.

She thinks for a moment before responding, "It's up to you, but I'd take time and think about it before you bring it up. He could be dangerous."

I end the conversation and try to process the information my mom has just given me. When I start to put the pieces together, it all makes sense.

When we first met all I could think about was how we were so alike. Both of us had red and black hair, we both had facial piercings, and we listened to the same kind of music. He was so my style it was crazy. It was almost like he was the boy version of me. But that was before things started to get fishy.

I remember when we got our school ID cards, his card said "Austin" instead of "Romeo." When I questioned him about it he said that when he got put into foster care, they had to change his name because it had something to do with the devil and since he was passed around through a church system, they had to change it. It sounded a bit suspicious to me, but I had no reason to assume otherwise. The more I thought about it, I realized that all of his stories were never told exactly the same way. Honestly, some of them were just not believable at all, like the story about his hair.

When he first started coming around, half of his hair was shaved. When he was asked about his style choice, he would explain that part of his hair fell out in treatment. He would say that he was lucky because instead of a painful reminder of his struggles, he had a cool new haircut. It never really made sense to me, how only the left side of his hair fell out. It looked to me like it had been shaved, but I could never get myself to call him out. After all of the questionable stories and over-exaggerated scenarios, I still would have never guessed he had made up his entire life.

I realize I've been standing here lost in my thoughts for almost five minutes. I take a deep breath and pull myself together. Slowly, I turn around and walk back to the group. Surprisingly, no one questions my extremely long phone call, but by this time I'm pretty sure I could have left without being noticed. As soon as I reach the group, I start to tremble.

My heart is pounding louder than my thoughts and I can't even look at him. Instead of taking my place next to him on the bench, I walk over to my best friend, Kayla, and ask her if she wants to go have a cigarette, doing my best not to let the group hear the anxiety that fills my throat. Before walking away again, I make sure to flash a smile to the group to kill any suspicion. But they are all too engaged in one of "Romeo's" crazy stories to notice.

As we turn our back to the group, I light the cigarette between my lips and inhale one long drag before passing it to Kayla. Wiping the sweat from my palms, I try to pull myself together.

"I need to talk to you," I say, this time letting my voice shake.

"What's wrong?" she asks. I can hear the worry in her voice. I catch her up on the situation and her jaw drops.

"OH MY GOD, what are you going to do?" she says. Her eyes widen, waiting for a response.

I close my eyes and take a deep breath. I do my best to block out the flood of emotions that have washed over me. "I have no idea, that's why I wanted to talk to you about it. Normally I would flat out confront him. But what if he really is violent?"

She pauses for a second. She looks puzzled, almost as if I had asked her to solve a riddle. When she finally replies, it comes out slow and quiet, "You still need to confront him, you can't pretend like you don't know. But I would wait until you are in a public place so that nothing can happen."

I think about her response and start to put together a plan. "Since both of us go to the same school but we don't have any classes together, why don't I confront him at lunch? That way he has the rest of the school day to calm down," I suggest.

"That sounds like a perfect idea," Kayla replies. "Just make sure someone goes home with you after school, because he will have to come get his stuff sometime."

Now that I am starting to get this mess figured out, I feel like I can breathe again. My heart rate slowly returns to normal. "What do I do until then?" I ask, realizing that today I still have to go home with him.

"We have to pretend like we don't know anything," Kayla says, firmly. "I'm spending the night so just stick close and it should all be okay." With that said, the cigarette is gone and we slowly turn back to the group.

To my surprise, they are all still oblivious to the situation. We walk back laughing and smiling to make it seem as if nothing is out of the ordinary. We can't handle him finding out sooner than we planned.

Blocking out the negative thoughts, I take my spot next to him on the bench and let my hand intertwine with his. I look him in the eyes and force a smile as he kisses me on the cheek.

❧

I want to close the door on all the lies, and open the door to a true reality.

A Note from Lilly

The next day at school I broke up with Austin through a letter explaining what I had recently found out. As soon as school ended, he came straight to my house and denied everything. I shut him down but let him stay one more night so he could figure out a living situation. Since then he has dropped out of high school and was sent back to Texas where he got arrested for abusing his mom. This situation really taught me to always trust my gut. If something seems wrong, take action because you are probably right. Now I am a sophomore at Scriber Lake High School and I'm on track to graduate early. After graduation, I plan to go straight into cosmetology school to get a job in hair and makeup. At some point, I want to go back to school to get my degree in business and hope to someday open my own salon.

SICK AND TIRED
OF BEING SICK AND TIRED

EMMA NORTON

"Give me the lighter!" Samantha says. I know that she's annoyed with me, but I have to think hard about it because meth and heroin make my head cloudy and there's pressure behind my temples.

I hand her my green scratched-up lighter. I don't say anything because I'm too busy trying to forget about my home.

All I can think about is my mom and her straight red hair, her green eyes with spots of amber in them, and my dad who I look exactly like, only smaller and feminine. My dog Bear is in my head. I can see him running around playing, the gray around his mouth and the giant tumor on his cheek. I think about my home—where I am loved and accepted no matter what—which I have abandoned to get high.

"Can you block the wind?" Sam says, unable to hit the bong.

"Yeah, come here," I say.

I listen to the water bubbling and smell the dank scent of smoke. I feel as if I'm in a trance. I pull out my neatly folded but used foil and lean my head back against the brick wall, right under a "no trespassing" sign. We are sitting on the cold cement up a few feet from the ground in what we call "the hole." How did we even find this spot? I know it's around the corner from a smoke shop. I don't know how we got here. Did we walk or take a bus?

I'm not even sure what time it is, maybe around two in the afternoon. I do know that it's Thursday because I've kept track of the days since we ran away.

Suddenly a car drives slowly past us. I didn't even hear it coming. Then I see that it's a cop. My heart drops, and it feels like it's pounding in my stomach instead of my chest.

I'm begging God in my head, *Please don't let him stop; don't let him see us.*

"Fuck, Sam," I say as we watch the cop drive back toward us.

"Act normal and play along, I'll do the talking," she tells me.

I look at the foil in my hand and try to memorize the black lines I formed into a design as if it's the last time I'll see it. Then I quickly shove it into my bra. Samantha shoves our pink Hello Kitty bong into the corner of the hole and I realize I'll probably never see that again either. I frown at it, and then I see that the bowl is still loaded. I grab the weed out before the cop makes his way around the car to confront us. I shove it in the pocket of my baggy, sky blue zip-up sweatshirt that used to be tight on me before I started doing heroin.

I feel like time is frozen and what is happening is not real, like I am in a dream. I look at Samantha and see the worry on her face. She has dirty blonde, wavy hair that barely reaches her collarbones. The left side of her head is shaved almost all the way back. Her eyes are huge. I know they are a piercing blue, but right now there is no color—they are just black. With mascara on, her eyelashes touch her eyebrows. She's small and appears to be innocent and scared. But she's neither.

A tall, thin cop approaches us. I can tell by his muscled arms that he's in good shape. He has a thick mustache and stubble on his jaw. He acknowledges us with that smartass look that cops have, like he's the coolest.

"You know, this is a no trespassing zone," he says.

Sam does the talking and I keep my mouth shut. "Oh, I'm sorry officer. We were just talking and didn't know it was a no trespassing zone."

She tries to sound sweet while standing in front of the bong to hide it.

"Please sit down on the edge of the wall," the cop asks with a hint of a demand.

We hesitate for a minute but end up following his direction. He sees the bong shoved into the corner and points to it, giving us a knowing look.

"That was here when we got here," Sam says quickly. "It's not ours. We were just looking at it." I can tell he isn't buying it from his hard eyes staring at us.

"It really isn't ours. There's not even anything in it," Sam says, trying harder to convince him.

He takes it and gives us a look like he isn't stupid. "Okay, well, I'm going to throw it away in that dumpster," he says.

"Wait, can I do it?" Sam asks.

I watch her walk to a big green dumpster and toss it in while I'm still sitting on the edge of the wall. I frown at the dumpster and forget about it.

For a moment I think the cop is just going to let us go. But then he asks for our names. We both sit there and say nothing as if we didn't hear him. He asks again. Still nothing. We just stare at the ground. He asks another time, trying to be polite, but I can hear the anger in his voice. This makes me a little happy. Sam shoots me an annoyed look, like she's giving up. She tells him her name and address, giving a sigh when she's done. Then he turns to me.

I take a deep breath. "Dammit," I say as I exhale. I tell him my name and he jots it down on his little notepad. Then instead of retreating to his car, he decides to keep his eyes on us and says our names in that weird cop code, to whoever is on the other end of the phone. I giggle a little.

The cop listens to the voice over the phone and looks at us. "You are both reported as runaways, and I'm to bring you both to the station," he says. By this point I've had enough and decide to cooperate with him.

"Running away and doing drugs really isn't the life you want to live," he warns us. What he doesn't realize is that our current lifestyle is a lot worse than that.

"How old are you girls, anyway?" he asks.

"Fifteen," Samantha and I both say at the same time.

I'm on my way to the police station in the back of a cop car. I had been missing home before, but now that I'm caught I realize I'm not ready to go back. Running away again and how I'm going to get my next hit is all that's going through my mind.

My dad arrives at the police station and gives me a big hug. I see that his eyes are glossed over, puffy and red. I can tell he hasn't gotten much sleep but he looks relieved. A pang of guilt strikes me. I want to cry, but I can't. I've only been gone for three days but I'm pretty sure he knows I've been using drugs.

The drive home is silent and awkward. I recline in the passenger seat, play music and try to relax. I feel like I'm going to vomit because my stomach is sensitive from the drugs, and the stale smell of pizza and garbage in the car is choking me. My dad isn't all that focused on driving; I can see him looking at me through his peripheral vision.

"I hope you know how hard it was to give your dental records to the police in case they found your body," he says finally.

I don't know how to respond, so I say nothing.

When we get home, I act like nothing has happened. I don't talk to my family. I just go up to my room, shut the door and stay there. I feel as if the heroin and meth are taking turns with how they make me feel. One minute I'm nodding out, and the next I'm running back and forth from my bedroom and bathroom, cleaning.

I don't feel right at all. I'm getting dizzy; my brain feels like it's spinning inside my skull. My heart feels like it's going to explode because it's beating so fast and hard. I'm really confused. I feel cold and sweaty and think I'm going to throw up. I Google my symptoms and they match up with an overdose. I don't think I'm overdosing though, because I think it would feel more serious. I want to make sure so I call my best friend, Chelsie.

I tell her everything that's going on, how I got back home and how I don't feel right. I'm sitting on my bed, my mind racing while I smoke a cigarette, trying to calm myself down. Chelsie tells me that she loves me and that I'm going to be okay. I push "end" on my iPhone and feel more relaxed now that I've talked to her. I light another cigarette, not caring about the rules in my house.

Both my mom and my dad burst into my room, making me jump because I didn't hear them come upstairs.

"ARE YOU HIGH?" my mom practically screams at me. "Chelsie just called and told me everything."

"No!" I bark back, because I suddenly don't feel high anymore. In fact I feel like I need more.

"What in the hell is going on?" my dad snaps.

"Can I just talk to Mom, please?" I ask. He frowns but accepts it and heads back downstairs.

I feel a lot more comfortable without my dad staring at me with all that disappointment in his eyes. I just want the warm coziness of my mom. I tell her about all the dangerous things I've done—all the drugs and strange people. I tell her what I feel like now. She comforts me instead of criticizing.

"Do you want to go to the hospital?" she asks calmly. "And what do you think about inpatient now?"

I hesitate because I just want to be with her. If I go to the hospital, she won't come with me because she has to work in the morning. Even though I'm a mess in the head from the drugs, I still have a heart. I miss my family and I feel guilty about putting them through all of this.

While my mom and I are talking, my dad calls 911 and a few minutes later, six EMTs arrive to take my vitals. All of them are staring at me. I'm starting to have a panic attack, retreating farther away from them and closer to the sliding glass door of my kitchen, refusing to let them touch me. I'm crying and shaking because there are so many people.

A bald EMT with glasses and a long, white coat that looks like it belongs to a scientist is the only one who will speak to me. "Your vitals are okay, so you can ride with us in the ambulance car if you'd like, or your dad could take you."

I choose my dad but I start to have another panic attack in the car because I feel so uncomfortable in my own skin. My mind is racing. I'm confused and lost. My dad is crying while he's driving and he gives me a cigarette. "You can smoke it in the car," he says. He only smokes when he's stressed out, and I know he only has cigarettes because of what I have been doing. Another pang of guilt strikes. I can't do this anymore. I can't hurt my family like this.

I get to the hospital and I'm immediately rushed into a bed. The nurses do more tests and tell me I'm just having really bad withdrawals. I let out a huge breath, like I've been holding it in for hours. I feel relief and find comfort in the hospital bed with the warm blankets and fluffy pillows.

I didn't think that coming down was going to be this bad. Only two options are playing through my mind: either I'm going to be high 24/7 or get clean.

I'm lying in the hospital bed, thinking really hard about this. Because of the meth, I have chewed a hole in the inside of my cheek. I couldn't feel it, though, until the meth started to leave my body and it's one of the worst pains I've ever experienced. I'm so dehydrated that the inside of my mouth feels like it has been dried out with a towel. I have to get an IV, which I hate. The thought of a needle inside of my vein makes my heart jump.

I'm resting my eyes and hear the curtain to my room open. I look up and see my mom. I almost don't believe this because she has work in the morning. I'm surprised and happy. I smile the first genuine smile I've had in days and I make my decision.

"I'm ready, Mom," I say to her. "I'm ready to stop this. I'm truly sorry for all I've put you through and I want to go to inpatient."

I see my mom looking down at me with the IV and all the wires. I see the tears in her eyes. She squeezes my hand and smiles.

❧

I want to close the door on my drug use, and open the door to a new, healthy and successful life.

A Note from Emma

This occurred on May 2nd, 2013, and I headed to rehab the next day. I have been clean from heroin and meth ever since. I relapsed on weed, but I have been clean since August 9, 2013. My addiction got in the way of my high school education, and I didn't finish my freshman and sophomore years because of it. I am a junior now and I'm looking forward to finishing this year successfully. With the help of Scriber Lake, I will be graduating on time next June. My goal is to go to the University of Washington to become a veterinarian and to remain clean and sober. I have to take it one day at a time in order to succeed.

RECKLESS

CHASE WERNER

The hairs on my forearms are standing up from the chilly air that circulates through the crevices in the antique floorboards of my rented bedroom.

I weave the loose matted carpet through my toes as I look down at the final settlement documents from my mother's passing. It seems as if all the emotion I have held inside me from that day two years ago has decided to make one last attempt at ridding my mind of what sanity it has left.

As I begin to lose myself in the plethora of pages, I feel the crushing sorrow and regret that has been haunting me for two years now press against my chest. It's like a horror movie replaying over and over in my mind. And once again I'm back to that day in the third floor apartment where I last felt the comfort of home.

❧

The soreness I felt from my eyes getting the first stretch of the day made me realize that I hadn't gotten much sleep the night before. I turned my head and looked at the clock sitting on top of my makeshift mini-fridge nightstand. It read 7:45 a.m., an hour and a half past the time I was hoping to see.

"Oh shit," I said, jumping out of bed.

I threw on an outfit and rushed down the hallway. I had been late more times that year than the rest of my total education combined and I had to be on time.

I heard an exasperated call coming from my mother's bedroom. "Chase?"

I was so close to leaving my apartment. I knew I had no time to waste.

"Chase?" she called again.

I felt my body tense. I figured this was just some form of front she was putting up, like when she would miss work and have me cough into the phone to prove that her son was sick. Or when we couldn't have something we wanted for Christmas because she said the IRS had messed up on our taxes that year.

I didn't have time for this today.

Frustrated, I hurried to her bedroom and found her lying on her bed in an awkward position, like she had attempted to get off the bed and failed. Next to where her head was positioned, I noticed a red stain on the mattress sheet. I assumed it was blood from a gum disease that we both suffered from. My mother glanced up at me with a pleading look, as if I was her only chance of getting out of the bed.

"Can you help me to the bathroom?"

Her words alarmed me. She had never asked me to help her to the bathroom. But the clock also alarmed me. I had to get going or I was going to miss my bus.

I helped her out of her bed. My shoulders supported her entire body weight—her arm hoisted around the left side of my neck as I carried her gently to the bathroom and sat her on the toilet. A wave of concern rippled through my body. For an instant, I considered staying home and taking care of her because something was different this time. I had learned from experience that when things started to become different, it meant a lot of changes ahead. But my mother had been through a lot in her life and I figured she could make it through this, too. I had to get to school. I shot her a concerned look and briskly walked out of my apartment without even saying goodbye. I raced across the street where I barely caught the city bus to school.

I made it to my classes on time and forgot about the morning at home. At lunch Brytan, a friend of mine, asked me to hook him up, so he quickly drove us to my apartment.

I smelled something putrid the minute we stepped through the door. I had never smelled anything like it.

"What's that smell?" Brytan asked, waving his hand in front of his face.

I ignored him and tried to ignore the smell because we were in a rush to make it back to school in time for fifth period. We quickly headed to my room. As we walked through the hallway, I shouted to see if anyone was home, but there was no reply. I figured my mother was out.

We left shortly after and made it back to school just in time for fifth period. I had made arrangements to catch a ride with Brytan after school so I wouldn't have to catch the bus home. He dropped me off at a corner store up the hill from my apartment where I ran into my friend Jimmy. We walked down my hill toward the entrance of my apartments. That's when I saw the ambulance. Suddenly I knew.

"I think I my mom is dead," I said, turning to Jimmy.

"Should I leave?" he replied.

"Yeah man, I think that would be best."

Crossing the lot to my apartment, I couldn't seem to find a feeling. My body was numb as I approached my home, waiting for confirmation of what I already knew in my heart. I headed up the stairs to the top porch where two paramedics, my auntie, and grandmother greeted me.

"Do you want me to tell him?" the paramedic asked my aunt.

She reluctantly looked at me, water streaming down her face. "Your mother is no longer with us," she sobbed.

My body felt as if the plane of existence that I had been living on had switched. I felt lost. I couldn't believe this was true reality. There was no way my mother—the only person who has ever stuck around—had been removed without a moment's notice. It was so unexpected that for a minute I was too stunned to think. My numbness was quickly replaced by fear. All that was suddenly running through my head was that I had around eighteen ounces of weed in my bedroom, which represented my only chance of surviving on my own.

"Can I go inside?" I asked the paramedic, trying to keep my voice calm.

"Is that something you think you can handle, Chase?" my aunt quickly interjected.

The paramedic opened the door part way. Through the slit, I could see a white apparition on the floor that didn't belong in the center of our living room. By the time the front door was fully open, I could see her lifeless body covered in a white shawl from head to toe.

I stepped inside, stood at her feet and looked down at her for a few seconds, trying to comprehend what I was seeing. Then I remembered what I had to do.

"Can I go my bedroom?" I asked the paramedic, still fighting to keep my voice steady.

He told me I couldn't because a person called a coroner was going to come to my home and analyze everything, so everything had to be in the exact condition it was in before the paramedics arrived.

"Please? Just for a minute. I need to be alone," I asked again, trying not to sound desperate.

"No, I'm sorry," the paramedic repeated.

I walked through the remainder of my living room to the entrance of the hallway where my mother's bedroom glared at me. It was the location of the last memory I had with her. I couldn't seem to find a solution. My mind was so lost. I walked down the stairs to where the grey square of pavement signals the beginning of the black top parking lot. I walked drudgingly towards the opposite side of the lot so that the paramedics couldn't hear my thoughts. I've always been easy to read and I didn't want to make it apparent that I was stressing about what was in my bedroom.

I looked up at the third-story window with the light on. I knew that as soon as the coroner opened the door to my bedroom, all he would see was a copious amount of marijuana on my coffee table. At that point it would be over, and the worst day of my life wouldn't only be imprinted on my heart, but also in my legal records.

I decided right then and there that I would do anything within my power to avoid getting arrested. My grandmother couldn't stand to be inside the apartment, so she stood outside at the bottom of our steps. I watched her cross the parking lot to join me.

"Are you okay, Mijo?"

I didn't know what to say so I just cut straight to the point. "Grandma, I got some stuff in my room that I don't want the coroners to find but the paramedics won't let me go in."

My grandma looked at me with a mix of surprise and disappointment. "What kind of stuff is it, Chase?"

"It's just weed."

My grandma turned around without saying a word and headed up the stairs to the apartment. Shortly after, I saw the light in my bedroom vanish. I waited for a moment until my grandma came down the stairs and walked towards me, away from the paramedic.

"I took care of it," is all she said.

I had nowhere else to go so my grandma invited me to stay with her.

That evening was a blur. I was still too stunned to feel much of anything. The next day she flushed my weed down the toilet.

❧

I'm in the room I've been renting from an elderly couple for the past nine months—living alone while working as a baker at a nearby teahouse and trying to finish high school.

I watch my tears hit the settlement papers and quickly move them so they don't get wet. The questions I've been asking myself for the past two years swirl in my head.

Why didn't I stay home that day? Why didn't I do more to help her? Why didn't I tell her I loved her? Why is it that you never realize what you have until you lose it?

I've had plenty of time to think about the things I would tell her if she was still here. I would thank her for everything she did for me, and for being the only support and one constant in my life. I'd tell her how many things have changed for me and where things are headed. I think she would be proud if she could see me now.

I stare back down at the settlement papers one more time. I quickly scrawl my signature in the marked places, shove the papers into the envelope and lick it shut—and it feels like a final goodbye.

❧

I'm closing the door to doubt; I'm opening the door to enlightenment.

A Note from Chase

It's been two years since my mom's death and I'm working hard to move forward with my life. I no longer sell drugs and I'm now a senior, on track to graduate next year. I took cello lessons before my mom's death and am passionate about music. After graduation, I'm going to study music theory and audio engineering.

LOST RESPECT

BRINNON HALL

"Be on your best behavior. Be respectful to me and dad," my older brother, Brad—my dad's favorite son—says as we're pulling off the freeway.

I can hear his cold, assertive, asshole tone over the death metal blasting in my ears.

"Huh? You say something?" I spit out, pretending I didn't hear him.

"You heard me, you worthless waste of space," he spits back.

I feel my rage starting to boil.

"I'll behave, but I don't have to respect you, because you don't respect me. That's how it works," I fume, fighting to keep my voice steady. "And I don't have to respect that low-life fuckup. He's the one who made those decisions. He's the one who left us to fend for ourselves and he lost my respect a long time ago. Another thing: stop trying to control me like I'm your little puppet. I am old enough to do things on my own and make my own decisions. You can't just shove me around anymore."

He slams hard on the brakes and we slow to a stop. Before I have a chance to ask him if that was it, if we were just going to leave it there, my brother grabs the back of my neck and slams my face against the dashboard five times. Then he pins me to the center console and starts to pound on my face over and over again until the light turns green.

"YOU will respect me *and* him because he made you," he yells. "And if you don't respect us, I'll just beat it into you!" He smashes his foot on the gas pedal as he speeds towards another red light.

I sit up and flip down the visor, opening the mirror flap to examine the damage. A black eye is already starting to form. My nose is bleeding and my lip is swollen to three times its normal size—split right down the middle. *Whatever,* I think. *Go fuck yourself. Ignorant asshole.*

I stay quiet for the last fifteen minutes of the drive because I don't feel like being used as a punching bag again. It's hard to put up a fight against someone who's twice your size and is always jacked up on steroids and pain pills.

Brad is twenty-one years old, tall and heavy. He has short blonde hair, cold blue eyes, and a double chin covered by a stubbly blonde/reddish beard. He has a beer belly that sticks out a little bit past his waist, and biceps that are seventeen inches in circumference. Every day he wears a big silver "Ellensburg Rodeo" belt buckle, and his bottom lip is always packed full of Copenhagen Straight Long Cut Chew. When he smiles, his k-9 teeth look like small, white fangs.

I'm fifteen, 5'9", and thin, like a twig. I'm very scrawny.

We creep up the hill towards the little box that we speak into to tell the guard in the tower which building we're going to, the visitation hours we are here for, my dad's cell block number, and his inmate identification number. Once done, the guard tells us where to park and when the visitation starts, even though we already know.

We park and my brother tells me to leave everything in the truck except for my ID, the food card that the prison gave us six years ago, and any money I have to put on the card. I take everything out of my pockets, open the door and jump out.

As soon as my feet touch the ground, I think about the night after my dad got out of county jail. I was only four and had gone downstairs because I couldn't sleep. I saw my dad leaned over the kitchen counter snorting something.

"Oh shit," he said, looking up when he was done. "Hey, Brin. What are you doing outta bed, buddy?"

"Daddy, what are you doing? I can't fall asleep," I mumbled back.

"Nothin' homie. I was tryin' to open my beer, you want a sip?" I watched as he wiped the powder from the pill off the counter.

"Uuuh huh," I nodded.

I heard the tires squeal around the corner when I brought the bottle of ice cold Corona to my lips. I heard the gunshots start when the beer passed my lips, and heard the glass shatter when I started to swallow the first gulp. My dad was shot in the shoulder as the beer slid down my throat; when the bottle was parallel to the floor, it shattered in my hands as a bullet came within six inches of my face.

My dad dropped to the ground and clutched his shoulder to keep the blood from flowing out. I had glass in my hands, all over my face and in my mouth and eyes.

❧

"Brinnon, come on, stop fucking standing there like an idiot!" my brother yells at me.

Shaking my head, I slowly walk away from the truck and along the path toward the cold, hard concrete walls that hold the man I reluctantly call "Dad." We pass through the door and out of the snowy December weather, turn the corner into the door that says "visitation" and head up the stairs to give the correction officer behind the counter our information. Then we take a seat and wait for them to say his name.

After we get past the metal detectors of both steel doors controlled by the guards, we have to walk up to another guard who tells us where to sit while we wait for my dad to get strip searched before he finally walks out.

I spot him from the line of prisoners as soon as he steps through the door. His hair is buzzed, like usual, and he is extremely muscular. His biceps look like miniature boulders underneath his skin. He has golden hazel eyes, deep smile lines, and deep pockmarks all over his cheeks from years of popping pimples.

He checks in with the guard and then walks over to us. His abs feel like rocks up against my stomach when he pulls me in for one of his bear hugs. He sits down in the chair with the taped yellow stripe on it.

"So, how have you been, B? What happened to your face?" he says, motioning to my black eye and bloody nose.

"Uh, I could be better I guess. You? And nothing, Dad, I just fell out of the truck," I tell him, glancing nervously, worried about his response.

"Why could you be better, son? What's wrong?" he asks.

"If I told you what happened, it's just going to happen again as soon as we get in the truck." I look at my brother, who is glaring at me with a 'Do you really wanna get your ass beat again?' stare.

"Brad, what did you do to your brother on the way here?" my dad demands, looking straight into my brother's similar, manipulative smile.

"Nothing, Dad," I answer quickly before my brother can get anything out of his gaping mouth.

"Don't sit here lying to my face, Brinnon Walker," he says.

"Fine. Brad beat the shit out of me on the way here. Happy?" I tell him.

His body tenses as he says, "Really, Brad? I thought we were done with this shit. You're lucky I'm in here."

"You should've fuckin heard what he said!" Brad protests, sucking up to my dad like he always does.

❧

My thoughts jump back to when I was six, sitting on the couch in the living room as my mom danced around the house in a long, black sundress covered in large, yellow sunflowers. She was smoking a freshly sparked joint while blasting "Ashes" by Pepper.

"It's been so long and it's hard to breathe when the trust is gone," she sang. *"A face of steel just melts away in the weather. If you got a lot to weigh, just weigh it, if you got a lot to say just say it."* The phone interrupted her.

"Hello?" I heard her say while she held her hit in. Then, "You've got to be kidding me. I'll be there as soon as possible."

"Brinnon, Brad! Get in the van!" she yelled as she slammed the phone down. I could hear the terror in her voice as she screamed our names.

We piled into the van and sped off up our one-way street.

"What's going on, Momma?" I asked.

"We're going to get Daddy, sweetie," she said.

She skidded to a stop in front of my elementary school and then sped toward the freeway entrance. I looked at the speedometer—we were doing fifty in a thirty-mile-per-hour zone. She was still going fast as she swerved around the corner to get on the freeway, screeching the tires and almost rolling our blue Chevy Astro van off the side of the on-ramp into some trees.

I had never seen my mom drive like that before; my adrenaline was pumping through my veins harder than ever. A numbing, chilling sensation washed over me, like the feeling you get when you first jump into freezing cold water.

My mom quickly sped up to ninety-five, topping our heap of metal car out the whole way to Walla Walla without stopping.

She finally slowed down as we exited the freeway because there were police cars everywhere. I assumed they were looking for my dad. My mom sped back up once the coast was clear. We slowed down enough to take a sharp corner into a reddish-pink, U-shaped motel.

"Stay in the van, boys, I have to take care of your father," she ordered.

"Where is he, Mommy?" I asked.

"He's inside the motel room, sweetie. I'll be right back, I promise," she said, reassuring me that everything was going to be fine.

I watched as she walked through the office doors and spoke to the man behind the front counter. I saw him point to a room that was two parking spots away from ours, where I spotted our white Honda Prelude. I slid open the van door slowly so my mom wouldn't notice, hopped out and walked to the motel room window to see what was going on. I peered inside and saw my dad sprawled out on the bed with a TV tray in front of him. The way he was laying, it looked like he had been dead for hours.

I turned really cold again, like I was back in that lake.

I started to panic and began pounding on the window with all of my strength, screaming, "DADDY! DADDY! DADDY! Mommy! Daddy's dead!" I started throwing myself at the door to break it open. I heard the office manager rush over to open the door, my mom right behind him.

"Brinnon. Wait outside," she ordered.

I stood in the doorway, watching as she rushed through the door to my dad. She started shaking him and screaming, "Patrick, wake up! Fucking wake up! Start breathing!" She was sobbing and screaming, but he wasn't moving. I watched her drop to the floor. "He's gone! He's dead. I can't believe it. He's dead." She kept getting quieter as she repeated herself. After a couple of moments, all I could hear was her sobbing.

I shifted my body to the door next to my dad's room, slid down to my butt, buried my head into my knees and started bawling hysterically. I didn't know then that he had overdosed but would make it through. I thought he was gone forever.

❧

"What did you say about me and your brother?"

Hearing my father's voice snaps me back. I quickly glance at the clock. It's been thirty minutes. What have I been doing for thirty minutes? I hear the stern tone in my dad's voice as he repeats his question. It sets off an explosion inside me. I feel fire pushing the words out my throat.

"TWO LOWLIFE FUCKUPS," I start, surprised and happy to see the shock on my dad's face. "You want to know what I said? This is EXACTLY what I said. 'I'll behave, but I don't have to respect you, because you don't respect me. That's how it works.' Then I said, 'I don't have to respect that worthless pile of shit. He's the one who made those decisions, he's the one who left us to fend for ourselves and he lost my respect a long time ago.'"

My dad and brother are both just sitting there, staring at me like they've seen a ghost.

"Then I said, 'Another thing. Stop trying to control me like I'm your little puppet. I am old enough to do things on my own and make my own decisions. You can't just shove me around anymore.' Those were my exact words to the letter. Happy?"

Though I don't raise my voice, my tone is so lethal, vicious and threatening that I feel like venom is going to shoot out of my mouth any minute. Every second I sit there, the rage keeps building. After a minute or two, I'm so livid that all of my limbs are violently shaking. My legs can't stop bouncing. They are like two well-lubricated pistons inside of a motor, accelerating faster and faster, one after the other. They are shaking so hard that the table is scooting around. My fists are clenched so tight my knuckles are turning white. I feel my fingernails digging into my skin.

Calm down, I say to myself, *stop getting angrier. Please stop, please. You can't do this anymore, you can't take this anymore. Take slow, deep breaths. Slow your breathing down. Slow your breathing.*

They both continue to stare at me in shock. I see a mix of surprise, bafflement, and utter terror on their faces. I've never felt so good. I have finally put my foot down and now they're scared of me. For once in my life, I'm not the one who is terrified. Finally, the two biggest monsters of my bloodline are afraid, and it feels so damn good that it is me who has put the fear into their darting, bloodshot eyes.

"You know what. I have one more thing to say to both of you," I say as I glare into my father's eyes with so much intensity that he looks down at the table. He can't stare into my inferno because it's hotter than the sun. I make sure that he sees the pure disgust, hatred, betrayal, wasted years, loss of trust, and—overall —the fire roaring behind my dark blue eyes.

"You. You are the reason why I'm so fucked up. You're the reason why I have anger problems. Why I have such a thick wall blocking my emotions from the world. The reason that I crave drugs that I've never even had in my system! I'm glad you're locked up in here. It's where you belong. Here's a question for you to ponder. What's it like to be a complete failure?"

"And you," I maniacally hiss at my brother as I turn to face him. "Look at you. You're such a worthless fat piece of shit! Do you really think that beating me senseless every day made me grow up to be a good person? Do not ever think about reproducing. We don't need any more of your kind on this planet. And *boo hoo*. Your "back" hurts. You're hooked on those pills just like this fuckup over here. You won't admit it. I know that you are because I see you go through the same shit he did. Have fun being drug addicts you worthless space of two human beings. Have fun spending the rest of your life in here. Fuck both of you."

I'm done. I spring up and storm out the way I came, out the electronically controlled metal doors, down the stairs and out the door into the snowy December weather.

I quickly walk the long concrete path to the stairs and slide down the railing. As soon as my brother's blue Dodge pickup is in my eyesight, the inferno inside me explodes into an uncontrollable rage. I half speed walk, half jog towards his truck. When I'm about twenty feet away, I start sprinting. Before I can think about what I'm doing, my fist makes contact with his passenger door window and I hear the sound of glass shattering. I reach in, unlock the door and jump in to grab my shit.

I slam the door hard behind me, light a cigarette and inhale the fresh menthol smoke into my lungs. Then I start walking down the hill, away from the prison toward downtown Monroe.

I have closed the door on the darkest memories from my past. I'm excited to open the door to a fulfilling future by continuing to get good grades and graduating.

A Note from Brinnon

After I walked out of the prison that night, I stayed at a friend's house for a week or two. I didn't talk to my brother or my dad for seven or eight months. I recently started having awkward conversations with them every once in a while. One day I hope that my brother will stop treating me like I'm still five, but I doubt it will ever happen. This year is my second year at Scriber Lake High School and my grades are better than they've ever been, so that's something I have to be proud of. Though I still have a ways to go, I plan to graduate and go into the automotive industry—either as an automotive technician or working in the collision repair industry. One thing I've learned is that whatever negative things life throws at you, just say screw it and don't even let it faze you.

REPRESSED

ELIAUD PETERSON

Sitting at the end of the cold, hard bed I stare at the wall. I want to leave but the nurses' eyes are on my door.

The familiar smell of acidic hospital disinfectant fills my nose and makes me choke. I shift in the giant paper napkin, goose bumps rising on my skin from the cool air pumped into the room. I feel naked anyway, because I was stripped of everything "potentially dangerous" when I was admitted. I pull on my gown and try to cover my legs, but I know they have seen them and I don't like that. I don't let anyone see my scars.

A short, chubby male nurse walks in and says, "Do you want something to eat, sweetie? You're looking thin. You need to keep your strength up."

I ignore him. *Don't call me "sweetie,"* I think. *I don't know you.* My mind drifts through the fog of my day as my chest stirs in rhythm with the heart monitor next to me.

❦

I was walking down the hallway to my next class when my teacher saw me and thundered, "You. Get your ass to the office now!"

He said this loud enough for the other students to jump and look at me with wide eyes. Nobody liked him and most students were pretty scared of him. I wasn't, though. I could see through his authority complex and rudeness.

Without reacting, I turned to the office wing of the building. He hadn't liked me from the first day. He didn't like anyone who looked like me, talked like me, or dressed the way I did. All he saw was dark hair, clothes and a dim face. To him, I was a black smudge that could be removed and should be as quickly as possible. He demanded my respect and did nothing to deserve it.

I took my time getting to the office because I wasn't interested in what they had to say. I wasn't interested in much anymore.

As I stepped into the principal's office he held up a paper I had written. "You think you can get away with something like this, Peterson? That this would slip under our noses?"

It was my notes on glaucoma or something, but that wasn't what he was talking about. At the bottom was a note for the teacher. During his class he would teach until the last fifteen minutes and give everyone a break. Except me. He'd have me keep writing, even though I had nothing to work on. So one day I just wrote about him. I didn't see the big deal though; it was mostly a Monty Python quote.

I just stared at him as he read my comments out loud.

"Your mother was a hamster and your father smelled of elderberries. Your momma dresses you funny, you know that, and so what you decide to do with that leadless pencil you call an imagination is teach health?"

He sighed and looked at me with a glare of disapproval.

"This is disrespectful and threatening. He doesn't feel safe with you in his class, Peterson. Do you have anything to say before your mother comes in?"

I had to stifle a laugh. I was a ninety-eight pound, 9th grade girl and he was a grown man. *Fucking seriously?*

Again, I looked at him and said nothing. *This is gonna be loud,* I thought while waiting for my mom to arrive.

She walked in wearing sweat pants and a tank top. She wasn't even wearing a bra, and the only thing I could think was *sorry for disrupting your sleep, Princess.* I looked at the clock. It read 11:30.

"What do you think you're doing? What the fuck is this?!" my mom screamed, her face inches from mine. She did this a lot, asked questions without wanting an answer, just trying to get me to react. I wasn't going to show any emotion on my face or say I was sorry. Because I wasn't.

After a few minutes things got quiet. The principal took that chance to get a word in.

"Eli, because of the nature of the note and for your teacher's safety, we're going to have to emergency expel you. You'll have to leave the premises immediately."

I broke my silence.

"You have got to be kidding. You're expelling me for the last three days before summer break for this?" I said, disbelief falling from my lips. *Was this even legal?*

"It's not just for the remainder of the year. You can't come back here."

Wait. What? It took me a few seconds to process the absolute bullshit being thrown at me that I could do nothing about.

I never really liked my school. It had a lot of preps and teachers I had problems with. I knew I didn't belong there, but I didn't really care. I was done dealing with a school working against me, with kids who gave me shit for not looking like them, for not being a Barbie. I hated it.

"Excuse us. We need to speak in private," he said, swinging the door open and glancing at my mother, motioning for her to follow him to another room.

They left me in the office to space out and chew on my nails. After about ten minutes my mom came back in, grabbed my shirt and pulled me up, looking at me as if she was so done with me being her daughter. I had seen that look before.

Frustrated and angry, I stepped away and told her I was going to grab my stuff. Walking to my locker, I could feel her behind me. Her rage was tangible and I knew when we got in the car it was going to be audible, too. I would feel it on my skin and in my heart.

As we walked to her car, she grabbed everything in my arms, threw it in the trunk and yelled at me to get in. I hesitated, thinking, *What if I just ran off right now?* I almost did until she commanded, "Get. In." Her face twisted into one of hatred, her hair whipping across her face from the wind.

As soon as the car door closed, she started screaming and didn't stop. I was so used to hearing her high-pitched hollers that I could usually just tune it out. But not this time. I looked into her distorted, creased face and screamed back. I screamed until I had nothing left in me.

For months I had known that something was wrong with me. Ever since I was little I had experienced anxiety. After being admitted to the hospital for a broken leg when I was six, I started panicking over irrational things. My stress and anxiety affected me physically, landing me in the hospital multiple times for various sicknesses. But lately it had been getting much worse. I wasn't sleeping and I didn't go a day without intrusive thoughts that would bring me to the floor with my hands on my head, begging for them to stop. All of my memories were haunting me and I thought I was losing it. I let the walls fall down and would drown in my sadness and anger, sitting there sometimes for hours. I lost interest in everything I used to love—ballet, reading and writing. I just couldn't do it anymore. I started building walls from myself until I became comfortably numb and couldn't feel anymore. I still didn't care, but at least I wasn't hurting so much. I think the best part was that nobody noticed, because nobody seemed to care.

Those walls, though? Screaming and pushing my mom away in the car made them crumble to nothing. I was terrified of the anger and hate and rage I felt, but nothing was stopping it from coming out. I thought my chest was on fire.

Speeding home, my mom pulled up to the driveway. I ran inside, slamming the door behind me.

I bolted to my room and started screaming and throwing things. I grabbed my lava lamp I'd had since the third grade and threw it so hard that I thought I might have dislocated my shoulder. I watched it shatter and drip down my wall, remembering with satisfaction who gave it to me. Whipping my head to the doorway, I caught a glimpse of my mom before she closed the door behind her. It made me happy to see the fear in her eyes.

In that moment I honestly thought about dying and stopping it all. What was the point? This was hell. Why would I want to be in this world? I knew I could be successful at that and my mom knew it, too.

My mom was so scared that she hid in her room, not knowing what to do. She eventually stepped back out and stood in the hallway, just looking at me. She didn't seem to care anymore about me being expelled—all she saw was a shred of a girl, medicated and glued back together, being ripped apart by herself.

All the hate I felt in my heart, the sadness and the disgust, consumed me. I wanted my dad but he couldn't be there. I wanted a friend, but I had none. I wanted a mom who was a real mom. I wanted a home where I felt safe and loved and warm. I had nobody, I was nobody and finally every shitty thing I had repressed came up with the puke in the toilet.

My mom came into the bathroom, grabbed my arms and screamed, "Stop!"

I tried to get her hands off me because I hated it when she or anyone else touched me. But she managed to push me out of the bathroom. I tripped on the doorframe and we both came falling to the floor.

"You need to stop! Goddammit, Eli!" she shouted in terror and anger, her eyes wide and unreadable. All I could do was sit crumpled on the floor, crying. It was the first time in years I had let anyone see me cry and I felt violated. I felt naked and it just made me cry harder until I felt tremors shake me from the core.

"I'm taking you to the hospital. I don't know what to do. They can deal with you," my mom whispered to me, looking lost. I sat there staring at the wall, trembling, my jaw clenched.

We rode in her ugly red Honda Civic. I stared out the window and felt tears roll down my cheeks and my nails digging into my skin. I tried to focus on not crying. Not panicking. They would check me out and say, *Oh you're okay, just take this and it will calm you down.*

Take this for the pain.

Take this for the anxiety.

Take this to feel better.

No wonder I had started popping. I had been taught since a young age that pills fix everything. And, baby, I knew they would.

Pulling up to the emergency entrance, I saw the sign staring down at me. I hated hospitals so much and I knew I was going to be there for a while.

How would things be if I had never started cutting, pushing away my emotions and bottling them up with pills and painkillers and chasing them with booze?

I had killed all of my memories of abuse and pain along with the parts of my brain that showed me how to love. I wished I had someone to reach out to, but I had distanced myself, staying committed to the idea that I'd be rejected. I had always been told I was nothing, that I was defective, and I silently let these people morph my idea of self-love into self-destruction.

I could feel panic rising from the pit of my stomach. This was the place of my nightmares and memories. I took slow steps toward the hospital entrance, not feeling my hands or legs.

❧

I want to close the door to negativity and intrusion, and open the door to where "love is my weapon."

A Note from Eli

After my night in the emergency room, I was transferred to a psych ward for ten days. I did everything I could to get out of there, even pretending I was okay. Even though I was there for less than two weeks, when I stepped outside it felt like I hadn't felt the sun on my skin in years. Honestly being there didn't help me much, other than that I realized I had to be the one to work through everything. I'm still in the process of doing that, too, but everything takes time. I've been clean of cutting and painkillers for two months now and hope my story can help anyone in the situation I was in. I realize that life is both beautiful and ugly, but when you focus on the negative things, all the bad can take over your way of thinking and eat you alive. Sometimes all it takes is to look at the stars and moon to remember your problems aren't as big as they seem and you need just to breathe and make the first move in a different direction.

thank you for everything,

Stay beautiful!

x

Eli Pedersen

LOSER, FAILURE, DUMBASS

MAIZE PHILLIPS

"Hey guys, look! There's Maize! The class retard!" Kristopher Clayman screams out loud enough for me to hear two blocks away. The laughter surrounding him drowns him out for a moment. "Do you think he'll ever be smart enough to know that he might as well just die because he's so fucking worthless?"

Kris has been doing this for the entire school year. My hands are clenched into fists and I want to cover his face in scars. I want to destructively injure him, but leave him alive just so I can make him suffer more. I want to burn his skin off with my rage and break out his teeth with my fists. I am shaking with anger and I think I am going to lose control.

As the laughter continues, a couple dozen people participate in Kris' taunts. "You are so fucking stupid, you motherfucking dumbass!" they chant like some sort of choir.

Everyone on the curb is laughing. It is no longer just Kris that is pissing me off, and I want to hurt him even more because of this. I'm red in the face and my palms are sweaty. My heart is thumping against my rib cage, making me feel like it's going to jump out of my chest like the alien organisms in the Aliens vs. Predator movies. My body is experiencing an internal earthquake. The ringing in my ears makes me think that they might bleed.

I'm not looking at him, but I'm sure he's probably wearing his usual red plaid, button-up dress shirt and jeans with sneakers that are worn way past their due date. He's probably smiling with his Jack Nicholson Joker smile. And, of course, I'm sure he reeks of marijuana.

I want to walk the eight hundred feet back to my school and kick his ass. But I don't do anything, I just walk home.

※

I knew that something was up when my 6th grade math teacher scheduled an appointment for me and my mom.

"Your son, Maize, has been diagnosed with ADD, ADHD, and a little bit of Autism Spectrum Disorder. But there's not enough for it to be obvious," Mr. Randy told my mom. He was an awesome teacher; I just didn't want to be there.

"What's Autism?" I leaned over to whisper to my mom in confusion. I knew what ADD and ADHD were, but I had no clue what Autism was.

She waved at me, signaling me to stay silent. "Does he need any medication? He was on something called ... was it Vyvanse?" she said as she turned to me. I was hesitant to say 'yes' because I hated being on medication—everyone expected me to be perfect when I took it. I didn't want others to have high expectations of me because whenever I did my best, it was never enough.

I nodded quickly and started to protest, "But you said you –"

She waved to cut me off again.

When I had come back from my dad's house in Shoreline, Washington, I begged my mom to let me stop taking Vyvanse. I told her how it builds unachievable expectations for other people in my life. I wanted to remind her of her promise that I wouldn't have to take it.

"I didn't say that you were. But you have to promise me that you'll be a good boy and at least try whatever he suggests," she said. I always felt a sense of comfort and relaxation whenever she patted me on the leg and said 'good boy.' I nodded to show that I was willing to try whatever Mr. Randy suggested.

I zoned out when they continued to talk about my IEP and how to start. All that I got out of the conversation was that I was 'special.' And 'special,' to me, meant that I was stupid.

❧

I throw myself against the couch and drop my backpack and coat next to the sliding glass door. I'm sick and tired of this bullshit; it has gone on for far too long. I shake with anger, believing that my rage can shake hell through the cracks of the earth.

Why does it always have to be me who gets pushed around by assholes like Kris? I think to myself. *When I get made fun of by an entire school every fucking day, do my parents actually expect me to just sit back and ignore it?*

I haven't been pushed over the edge like this for three years. I can feel myself transforming, my fuse getting shorter every time it happens. This feeling that is building is a destructive recipe, and aggravation and rage are the main ingredients. It's called hatred and it's building a will inside of me to do whatever it takes to make this shit stop.

As I sit in my rage, I feel my blood vessels bulging and know my face is turning bright red. My nails dig hard into my palms until they bleed. I think back to when all of the name-calling started three years ago, in the fifth grade at Echo Lake Elementary. Isaiah, the class bully, took many of my friends away and turned them against me. My cousin, Jared, and I used to hang out together. He never participated in Isaiah's bullshit, but he never stood up for me, either, which made him just as bad in my book. All Jared did was just ignore that the bullying existed. He was a bystander.

My little sister, Lillie, slides the glass door open, entering both the house and my furious anger.

"Hi Maize!" she exclaims. She always comes home with excitement in her voice, laced with a hint of deception. She makes you think she is a sweet girl and then, when you least expect it, she irritates you to your breaking point.

"Hey Lillie," I answer without emotion. Usually I'm excited to see her, but not after what just happened. The last thing I want right now is to be annoyed even further.

I think of what I want to say to my family.

You don't understand what I've been through. If only you all knew my pain, you all could help me escape from this hellhole. I wish I could just tell you, but my will is too strong to allow that. What's wrong with me? Why can't I just tell you guys?! What if Isaiah and Kris are right? What if I actually do screw up everything?

God, help me! Take me back to Calvary Chapel Lynnwood; bring me back to church, where I am respected for who I am, where I won't have to deal with all of this.

"Whatchya doin'?" Lillie asks, knowing it will annoy me. Although she doesn't know what just happened, I know she can see the aggravation in my eyes.

"Not now, okay? I'm not in the mood!" I exclaim loudly.

I admit that it is a little more than she deserves. Lillie doesn't use words to respond, her wide eyes amplify her glare. Her mouth gapes and her finger points at me as if I have just committed a murder.

My mom walks into the living room with anger pulsing through her veins. "What's going on here?"

She glances at Lillie and then her eyes dig into mine.

Oh, shit, I think to myself.

"I ... I ... uh ... I," I stutter, putting my hands in my pockets to keep them from shaking. My soul freezes and sends chills through my skin, making me break out in goose bumps. I feel the color drain from my face.
"I-"

"Maize yelled at me!" Lillie cuts me off in a bratty tone.

"Maize Caylob! Why did you do that?" my mom demands.

Do you want to know? Do you really want to know why I'm so short-fused? I think.

I mutter some stupid excuse because I'd rather just take the pain and get it over with than have to tell anyone what happened. I don't want to tell anyone because they would ask me how I feel, and I don't want to go there.

To escape the situation, I head to my room where I lie down and revisit my day in my head. It is filled with so many mistakes.

Mistake One: letting Kris' words get to me. Mistake Two: letting the feeling they gave me control me. Mistake Three: snapping at Lillie. Mistake Four: hiding my feelings so I had to bottle it up even more.

Why can't I do anything right?

Tears pour down my face. I am tired of being called a loser by kids. I am tired of being called a failure by schools and I am fed-up with everyone calling out to me like I'm a dumbass.

I stand, still shaking with anger, and wipe the tears from my eyes.

I think of a saying I once heard: "You are in control of your own life. You really do choose where you go in life."

Could I be in control? I wonder. *What if I haven't actually been trying? What if I work harder than I ever have? What if I prove those people wrong? Why don't I just try it? What do I have left to lose?*

✄

I want to slam the door on a life full of pain, anger, and failures.
I want to open the door and welcome a life full of fresh starts and respect.

A Note from Maize

This specific event happened when I was in eighth grade, motivating me to go from a 2.9 GPA to a 3.9! I started really caring about school. My 'disorders,' became pro-orders; they now help me with school. I would not have been able to prove those people otherwise if it weren't for my savior, Jesus Christ, my therapist Dr. Barrios, my friends and family, and Scriber Lake High School for giving me the chance to change myself. Without these people, I never would have a thriving GPA or a better personality. And this message is for all people: This story is proof that your life really is in your hands. All of you will find struggles in life, but you will overcome them. I plan to graduate early, become a diesel mechanic and make a band with my best friends. My stage name will be Xavier Alexander.

"You cannot control anyone's life but your own, but you can decide whether or not to make that person's life easier or harder. Minor difference and major difference is all the same."—Xavier Alexander

CLOSET DOORS

BRIEAUNNA DACRUZ

"Bri, the parade is going to start soon. Let's get ready," Ellen DeGeneres says, smiling at me with her big, bright white smile.

"Okay!" I say, "I'll be right there!"

Ellen is my all-time idol. I often lie in my room and fantasize about life with her as my mom. Someone just like me. Someone who understands and someone I can be comfortable with. I think of what our life together would be like. I could go on her show and to LGBTQ parades. We could do it all.

But someone is whispering in my ear. "Brieaunna, get up. I'm not going to tell you again."

It's my mom, using her gentle-yet-frustrated voice, trying to get through to me. She's been saying the same thing every day. But I continue to ignore this tall, brown-headed, Juicy Couture-smelling woman to keep my fantasy world going.

In my world, I think the real me would be looked down upon with shame, as just a foolish mistake. I bite my nails as I look at the family pictures on the wall and think about what my mom would say if she knew.

"No, you can't be. That's not possible. I didn't raise a gay," I imagine her stern, serious voice saying.

Some days I fake illness. It's the easiest way to get out of anything my mom tries to make me do. Maybe she will finally catch on; maybe she will finally ask deeper questions about what is really wrong. I don't like to lie to her because she has never done anything but love me. Letting her down is the last thing I would ever want to do.

My dad is a different story. He always refers to stupid things as "that's gay" or "this is gay." He will be the one with the most hatred. He's gone most of the year, for months on end, which doesn't make it easy to tell him something like this. I've always been daddy's little girl, but not a girly girl. I always liked playing soccer with him, wearing my basketball shorts and my hair up in a tie.

I hear my mom on the phone downstairs. By her edgy tone, I can tell she's talking to my dad. I think about two weeks ago when he told my mom and me to leave.

✿

"Get out of my house!" he yelled at my mom in his deep, slurred voice, drunk when we arrived home after dinner.

As I hurried past my mom towards the stairs to my room, she said, "Go get your things ready, your aunt is on her way to come get you."

Whenever they fought, I learned to stay away, and sometimes my aunt was my escape. My mom must have called her this time. All I wanted to do was go upstairs and sleep, but instead I had to throw clothes in my backpack. I was worried about my mom and where she would end up that night.

I heard loud screams coming from downstairs and my heart started to beat frantically faster. Then I heard the door at the bottom of the staircase open.

"You're not going anywhere!" my dad yelled in an angry tone.

I was scared to go back downstairs because I had to walk both through and around them. I just wanted to get out of there. My parents bickered often, but I had never been around when it had gotten this bad. They always maintained their cool because they didn't want me to witness any of it.

I zipped up my backpack and put it on. The back of my legs were shaking and my body felt cold. I walked quickly down the creaky wooden stairs. I always hated them. They were like another member of our family announcing my presence whenever I left my stupid room. I just wanted to be anonymous.

My parents, still in mid argument, were standing at the bottom of the stairs. As I walked quickly past, my dad snatched my phone out of my hand. I didn't react. I just walked straight to the front door and outside.

In the midnight cold the thin layer of my basketball shorts and white t-shirt sent chills throughout my body. I waited there looking down my street, hoping my aunt would show up soon to rescue me. But the street was empty just like my emotions. I felt numb. I had no phone to call her, so I just waited.

I wanted to hear my mom's voice telling me what to do or to see my aunt's car coming to take me out of this mess. Then I heard the big *boom* of the front door slamming and turned around to see my mom walking quickly toward her car.

"Come on. Let's go. Get in the car!" she said. I could hear the fear in her voice.

My dad yelled after us. "Get out of my house and don't ever come back!"

❧

Maybe this is why I've hidden my sexuality for so long, I think to myself as I lie on my bed. So much has happened that I don't want to put more on my parents and family. This is why I am staring at my purple walls, letting my freshman year go to waste, letting my future go down the drain.

Sometimes I allow myself to hope the day I tell my parents will be the start of something amazing. They will allow my girlfriends to come over, they will accept me for me and stand up for me when the world comes crashing down on me. Life will be good again.

What am I thinking? That's a dream never bound to happen.

I'm getting ahead of myself, getting my hopes up for no reason. Then I think about the other side. The day I turn eighteen I might be with a man, just to be like everyone else that is considered "normal," making sure my parents, family, and friends aren't disappointed. Force something upon myself that everyone wants, just to make others happy.

I shouldn't put others in front of myself. I should stand up for myself and let it all out. I hate hiding. Hiding in the closet they say. It's not the way I should grow up.

I know lying here all day isn't healthy; I am dropping weight, I feel trapped. I feel like a shell of a person. I can hear my mom at the bottom of the staircase and thoughts rush through my head.

Okay, I'm tired of being scared.

Suddenly my thoughts make me feel courageous, but just as quickly my stomach drops in regret. I stand up, my upper body is shaking and it slowly progresses down through my legs.

Society, disappointment, hatred, disowning. More bad thoughts.

Tightly grasping my bedroom door handle, I pause, feeling the clammy stress sweat on my palms. I open the door and slowly make it to the bottom of the stupid stairs that tell my mom I'm coming. I open the staircase door.

It's now or never.

I know what has to be done in order to relieve my stress, but am I too scared to be myself? I grab ahold of the door handle and open it. I freeze when I see my mom staring back at me.

"What are you doing, sweetie?" my mom asks.

"Oh, nothing, Mom."

I stand in awkward silence, trying to grasp the words in my head so I can push them out of my mouth. At this point I am angry with myself. I know I am already in the mode of letting my secret out, I just don't know how. I turn towards the staircase door, my only means of escape. But then I hesitate.

"Mom, I need to tell you something," I blurt out. The moment I say the words I want to take them back, go back upstairs and hide in my room again.

"One second," she says and places the laundry basket down. "So what did you need to tell me?"

My eyes fill with tears, but I hold them back from dropping. My body starts to shake.

"Uh," I say quietly, out of breath, trying to push the words out.

"Have you been doing drugs? Drinking?" I have never heard my mom's voice sound so paranoid. I chuckle.

"No, Mom. I'm gay."

Time stops. It feels as if the response coming from her takes hours, but instantly she turns and looks at me.

"I know you are, honey. I've known longer than you."

My body relaxes with an instant sigh of relief. I cannot believe that this has just happened.

She gives me a hug. "Even if I didn't know, I would love and accept you for you. You just needed to figure this out on your own. Thank you for telling me."

I know my life has taken an amazing turn, but I am still scared of other's reactions.

"I love you," she says in a motherly tone.

I open the door to the staircase and smile. I know I can finally be myself. Maybe my life does have a future.

Now when do I tell the others?

❧

I want to close the door on my worries, shame, and doubt.
I want to open the door to acceptance and love.

A Note from Brieaunna

Things don't always go as expected; in my case, things took a turn for the better. I am now sixteen years old. Months after revealing my big secret, my dad found out. As much as I was worried, I got the best of reactions. He accepts me for who I am and the decisions I have made in my life. I'm now a sophomore and proud to say I am on track to graduate. I have come so far from my purple-walled room to where I am now. I have met many others in similar situations, and what I've learned is that holding things in never helps, but letting them out relieves a lot of stress. Now I feel I don't have to marry a man to be normal; I can be who I am with my support system. I hope that because of my story you can see the strength that comes from being yourself. The door to acceptance may have many barriers, but through love, openness and honesty, you can make it through to the other side.

Brieaunna Lacruz

Thank you for all of your
support I apreciate it ♡
WE love you!

MY YELLOW BRICK ROAD

ROBERT JEFFREYS

His chest is pushed out and his eyes burn brighter than the fires of hell. I have just returned from school and have walked into a ticking time bomb.

The anger between my parents is evident because my mom's voice sounds broken while my dad screams in rage.

"I am sick and tired of you nagging me and telling me how to run this family!" he yells.

My mom looks at him with regret. She always begins by fighting back, then retreats because she knows she won't win. I know how she feels. It's taken me a few years to understand my dad's fighting pattern. It's either articulate and calm, or belligerent. Never anywhere in between. Mostly, though, he is able to negotiate with us calmly, and I appreciate it when he treats me like the man that I am. But I know how my mom is feeling right now and I am tired of seeing her emotionally destroyed.

"Can you go to your bedroom to fight?" I belt out. As soon as the words leave my mouth, I know I've made the wrong move.

He turns towards me. "Excuse me?" he yells. I can see his anger building, "Why don't you go to your room? You cannot speak to me like that!" His eyes become more inflamed and lock with mine. I stare back with a mixture of challenge and defeat.

I know I'm going to lose, but the rage makes me stand my ground and say, "You tell me what to do all the time. So what's the difference?"

But as soon as I ask the question, I know what the difference is: he's my father.

His temper snaps. His hands ball into fists and in that moment I think he has forgotten that I am his son. That he loves me. His arm moves back and my world flips completely upside down as his fist flies forward and connects with my chest. The pain of the hit bounces through my whole body. My blood drains and my heart breaks into shards of broken glass. It feels like life has stopped.

I never considered the possibility of my dad hitting me before, so I look at him in disbelief while gasping for air, trying not to appear weak. I wipe away tears. His penetrating gaze tells me that I deserved what I got.

The pain is too much for me to handle, so I turn to walk away. He grabs my arm in an effort to keep this heated exchange going. He wants to be in control. But it doesn't matter to me anymore, so I shake off his grasp. I want to go away and never come back.

I run out the front door, zooming past my dad. As soon as I get to the street, I try to take another step but as I push my legs forward, they buckle. I fall to my knees as my body turns to jelly. My heart is pounding out of my chest. The pain of the hit is non-existent because the pain of my broken heart is too strong.

I close my eyes, trying to relax. I go to my one happy place—the one place I can always go to and feel safe.

When I was seven, I would walk off the school bus and up the hill to our street with my brother, Jon, at the end of each day.

As we crested the top of the hill I would see my mom. She would stand at the mailboxes in front of our red and white house each day waiting for us. As soon as I saw her I would throw my backpack onto my brother and take off running. My legs would propel me down the street, faster and faster, until I got close enough to jump into her arms for a big hug and smell her musty perfume.

I would usually ask her, "Where is Daddy at, Mom?" and she would most always reply, "Daddy is in the shop outback."

I would turn and push myself as fast as I could up our dirt driveway. With each stride my body filled with joy. The thought of jumping into my dad's arms was the greatest thought in the world. As soon as I reached the top, it opened up to the backyard filled with trucks, muscle cars and motorcycles. I would scream out, "DADDY!" through the big, wide-open red barn doors of the shop. He would come running out, his arms wide open, and I would leap into his chest. For those brief seconds it felt like nothing could ever hurt me. It was always the best part of my day.

One day he hugged me, set me down and smiled at me like I was the most precious part of his life. "Son," he said. "I love you. No matter where you go in this life, I will always be with you, for you are blood of my blood." When he spoke those few words, my body became warm and my whole world felt complete.

❧

I stand up in the middle of the street and try to regain my strength. I am afraid to go back, but I push the fear aside and turn around and make myself walk to the house.

I enter the front door to find my mom sitting on the couch. I am relieved because my dad is nowhere to be found. But as I think of how happy I am that my dad isn't there, I look over at my mom. Her eyes are swollen with hurt and sorrow.

"Your dad is just having a hard time because he lost his job and we have no money," she tells me as I take a seat beside her.

My heart sinks deep into my chest. I think about the last three years since my father has been out of work. He used to work in construction, and I knew he was the best of the best, the go-to guy for everyone. But the economy changed things and his job wasn't in demand anymore so he was laid off. Ever since, he's done odd-ball things and small jobs for friends to help bring in money for the family. We gave up luxuries like cable TV and eating out and started eating more soup at home. My mom cleaned houses and tried to work harder to stay up on the bills.

Sitting on the couch next to her, I see my parents in a completely different light. I'm realizing for the first time how hard it has been for them. They never sugar coated anything, but I know that they have tried to protect us from worrying.

I know that I have to be strong, despite the hurt I feel.

"Mom," I say. "You just wait. You hear? You just wait." I stand and walk toward my room with heavy footsteps. As I pass my dad in the hallway, I glare at him; we exchange an unspoken understanding about what has just happened. Closing the door behind me, I slowly sit on the corner of the bed, my body limp.

On the wall in front of me is a collage of pictures from my childhood. I focus on one in particular: I'm four years old, and I'm sitting with my family on a three-wheeler that my dad had built. I feel so removed from those carefree days.

Something is now very clear: I know I have to leave my childhood behind for the sake of my family. I have to stop playing sports and other things that require money. I have to give up all of my free time and find ways to make money for my family. I must do what has to be done.

I lift up my eyes and put my life into the hands of God. I ask for the strength to push on and the courage to forgive.

❧

I want to close the door to the hurt and painful memories.
I want to open the door to happiness and the land of milk and honey.

A Note from Robert

It has taken me some time, but I have found the happiness that I've been looking for. My relationship with my dad has been restored. We still have our tough times, but we are much stronger together as father and son through mutual understanding and love. My dad is my hero; he is the man I want to be. As for my mom, she has a heart of kindness and eyes of peace. She has given me the courage to push on and face my fears. Both of my parents have taught me how to live life to the fullest and they expect me to soar high with the eagles. In fact, with their support, I recently earned the highest Boy Scout ranking of Eagle Scout. I am on track to graduate and plan to attend The Motorcycle Mechanics Institute in Arizona to follow my passion for mechanics. Every day I thank the Lord for my family. The most important thing my dad ever told me was that I become more powerful when I give my power away.

Robert Jeffreys

- keepin on truckin

STAINED

JAYCEE SCHRENK

I see red and blue flashing lights through the stained glass insert. Seconds later, three police officers push through the door and head straight to my dad, who is standing next to me. He leans over and whispers, "Keep your fucking mouth shut."

A young male officer with dark hair addresses him. "Sir, we need to know what your daughter called for." But my dad doesn't say a word. He looks past him as if he's not even there.

I walk over to my mom, who is no longer crying. She's acting as if nothing has happened.

"Ma'am, will you tell me the story again? I've been here for domestic violence calls before," the overweight male officer says with a concerned tone.

I'm surprised at his words; I didn't know about these calls. My head gets cloudy as the salt water builds up in my tear duct. I knew my dad had a temper, but hearing the police officer say something about "violence" makes me feel unsafe.

My mom glares at him and shakes her head. "I already told you! I have no idea why she called! Kids are full of shit when they don't get what they want. Go ahead, ask her!" She points to me accusingly.

Her words feel like knives cutting into my skin. How can she stand there and lie by calling me a liar?

He ignores her and waves over a female officer with piercing bright green eyes. She steps close and crouches down. I start to move away and she says, "Hey now, you don't have to be afraid. Can you tell me what happened?"

Her voice soothes me, but I know that soon after the officers disappear, the feeling will vanish along with my privileges of having a phone, watching TV, and playing with my friends. I clench my fists and dig my nails into my palms. I'm sick of being afraid, so I decide to take the risk.

"My mom and dad hurt each other. Why do they do that, when they say they love each other?" I start to choke on my own tears. She hugs me softly and assures me that justice will be served. I'm confused; I don't know exactly what "justice" means. As I hear the click of the handcuff, I rip myself from her grasp and watch my dad as he is walked across the yard and guided into the police car.

I'm shaking uncontrollably. *What have I done?*

"Dad!" I yell after him. "Please don't go! I'm sorry, Dad. Don't leave me. I'm so sorry. I didn't mean to do it, Dad. Please don't leave me!" Tears dribble off my chin as I'm screaming out the front door.

"Baby girl, you are my princess, so that means I am the queen. And your father? He's nothing more than a bank account," my mom said in her high-pitched voice as she hopped out of our silver Saab. I watched her walk to the cash machine in her dark-washed destroyed blue jeans and white flowing tank top with white flip-flops to match. I knew my mom was beautiful for her age; her style was plain, yet flashy. Her fingers were full of diamond rings, her wrists glinted with Coach bracelets, and ruby red earrings dangled off her ears. She returned to the car with stacks of hundred dollar bills—money to take me summer clothes shopping.

We ran up and down the mall from store to store, my hands holding multiple shopping bags. I felt as if my head was about to explode from the thrill of getting whatever my heart desired. I knew that most 6th graders in my class could never do this. I also knew that my mom had a bad problem with money and our monthly shopping trips were a secret between us. I always felt guilty but my dad rarely ever noticed.

As I placed my stacks of clothes on the Pac Sun counter, I shot a guilty glance at my mom to make sure it was OK to buy everything I wanted. But she reassured me with a kiss on my forehead and handed the cashier four hundred dollar bills.

"Have a nice day, because I know we will!" she said, flashing him her award-winning smile. She had been unemployed for seven years and didn't seem to care about the stress she caused my father as the breadwinner of the house. This was her third day of a three-day shopping spree and grownup, all-night parties.

I looked up to my mom; everyone seemed to enjoy her presence. Her laugh was contagious to most everyone she surrounded herself with, maybe because most of her friends were ganja enthusiasts or cokeheads. Even though she had puffed or snorted away her brain cells, I thought my mom was intelligent.

We skipped to the car, giggling and holding hands. I stuffed the back seat with our purchases and we headed home.

My dad was waiting for us when we pulled into the driveway. As he approached the car, I noticed that his hands were clenched and that his face was bright red. He still wore his mechanic work uniform with his nametag attached.

"Jenna, are you kidding me? $20,000? This is the second time in two years that you have done this to me, to us, to your children! Did you have fun going out to the bar last night and snorting some blow with your slut friend, Teri? Huh? Are you really that selfish? We are going to lose the fucking house! Give me it, give me the god damn money now!" he screamed.

I stood behind my mom, covering my face as I began to sob. I knew this fight would escalate because it had many times before, so I tried to be a distraction by crying louder. My dad crouched over, grabbed my forearm and dragged me across the pathway of our lawn.

My mom trailed behind us, screaming, "I didn't do anything, Doug! I don't know what you're talking about! Leave her alone!"

I could feel his muscles tense as he clamped tighter on my arm. His walking turned to stomping as he guided me over to the black leather couch in front of the TV, grabbed the remote and cranked up the volume. He headed out the back French glass door and slammed it shut.

I quickly turned off the TV so I could listen to their conversation, but I could only see their lips moving through the glass door. Then I saw my mom's face turn red and watched as she snapped her Channel glasses in two then threw them at my dad's head and ran for the door.

He followed her and his icy blue eyes locked with mine when he entered the room. I could tell by his vicious glare that I was not welcome.

"Go to your room, luv. And don't come out until I come and get you," he said in a voice that warned me not to disobey.

I headed to my room on the opposite side of the house and climbed on the desk in front of my window, planting my body on top. I gazed out at our front yard, wishing I was outside playing instead of stuck in this muggy room. I thought about all of the things I could be doing on a hot summer's day like this. *Maybe if I scrounge up a few dollars, I could buy ice cream cones and we could go to a park and play,* I thought to myself. *And maybe Dad would want to come if he isn't still mad at me.*

I slid off the desk and stepped towards my armoire, opened the door, and pulled out my underwear drawer. I dug towards the bottom until I felt the smooth glass of my piggy bank. I was fumbling with the cork, trying to pull it out, when I heard a loud thud.

I jumped on top of my desk again and got to my window in time to see my mom's body burst through the front screen door. She smashed onto the railing—almost flipping over it—and fell to the ground.

My hands went numb. I dropped my piggy bank and heard it shatter on my hardwood floor. Then I heard my mom's shrieks.

"DOUG, STOP!" she screamed, followed by more loud thuds.

In my hurry to get to her, I forgot about my broken piggy bank. I jumped down from my desk and landed on the pieces of glass. I felt a sharp pain as shards of glass sliced into the bottom of my feet, but I ignored it and bolted to the living room.

I stood frozen as I saw my mom lift her leg in the air and viciously slam her foot into my dad's rib cage. As he threw another blow, she retaliated by kicking his hand away from her body.

Something made my dad notice that I was standing there. I heard him gasp and say, "Oh, shit."

I knew my dad hurt my mom, but I had never witnessed it before. I had only heard her cries late at night. But whenever I hurried to her room to see what was wrong and comfort her, she would always send me back to my room saying, "You have school in the morning, go to sleep."

My dad tried to carry me away from the scene, but I panicked and thrashed my body around until I felt my feet touch the ground again. I ran into the kitchen, picked up my cell phone and dialed 911. As I fought away from him, he tried to rip the phone from my hand. I saw my escape: the front door.

I ran out, skipped down the stairs and sprinted up our street toward my neighbors' house. Don was like a grandpa to me. Anytime I didn't want to be at home, he would let me come over with my siblings and we would play cops and robbers at his house. I pounded on his door but there was no answer. I knew that he was a police officer and that this was his job. I needed help. *Where was he?*

I was too upset and overwhelmed to explain the situation to the 911 operator when she asked why I was calling. All I could do was repeat my address over and over again.

"Get her the fuck off the phone, Jenna!" my dad yelled. I didn't realize that my parents were right behind me.

I turned around and looked into my mom's red, puffy eyes. I could feel her fear. She grabbed the phone out of my hands. "I have no idea what she's talking about," I heard her tell the operator. "Please, don't come. We're fine."

The betrayal I felt was unexplainable. It was if I was on my first roller coaster; everything was going too fast to comprehend. I felt my stomach lurch into my throat, choking me and making a huge tangle of organs and intestines. *How could my mom tell the operator I was a liar?*

I stared at her bruised, swollen eyes. I looked at her knees that were still bleeding from skidding across the wooden porch and tried to register it all in my mind.

❧

"Don't worry. Everything's going to be okay," I hear the female officer say as the other officers push my dad into the back of the police car. Then they're gone.

I close the door, lock it, slide back against it and sob. So many emotions are swirling inside me. I feel so guilty for getting my dad arrested and taken away from us. And I know my mom's angry with me. But I also don't know what I did wrong. I thought I was supposed to call for help when there was trouble.

I look up and see my mom glaring at me.

"What?" I ask, hoping she hears the hurt in my voice.

"You don't understand what you just did," she says, flatly. Her neck has a red ring around it from where my dad choked her and her right eyebrow is split, blue and swollen. But there is no emotion on her face. "We have to do something, go somewhere. He'll be out by tomorrow morning."

That's when it hits me: she's scared of what my dad's going to do when he's gets home. And now I'm scared, too.

I know we've got to get away. My mom needs help and I have to protect her. Suddenly I have an idea. I jump up and race to my room, gather the coins on the ground and count them out: five dollars. Five dollars to live on for who knows how long. After all of our shopping excursions, I know that five dollars isn't that much. But it's what I have. I grab my Disneyland suitcase, stuffing all I can fit into it.

I hurry back to the den; my mom hasn't moved. She's in a fetal position, rocking back and forth.

"Let's go," I say firmly. "We have to go to Teri's."

She nods, looking past me.

"No. Come on, Mom. Let's go!"

I can see that my words are starting to register. I pull at her arm and she finally stands up. Then she grabs her purse and we both head to our car to start driving toward our new life.

❧

I want to close the door to the painful memories that keep me up late into the night. I want to open the door to a blissful, meaningful future full of laughter and love.

A Note from Jaycee

After three years of being in my mother's custody and trying to get her clean from heroin and meth, I realized that living with my grandparents was my best option. I've been with them now for two years. My mother is a recovering addict; she is two years clean as of next August. My father has gotten help and has not had a violent outburst in five years. I am proud to say that people can change— if you give them a reason to. After a few years of running from my demons and battling substance abuse, I turned to face them. I have fought the battle of my subconscious and won. I no longer dwell on or blame myself for the past, nor do I hold anything against my now-divorced parents for exposing me to the experiences that have haunted me in my sleep, keeping me awake for most of the night wondering 'why us?' I hope anyone who feels the need to speak up, will. I am now seventeen years old. My main focus is school, because I will soon be graduating and heading off to twelve more years of school to become a psychiatrist. I want to be the ear someone like me can whisper their thoughts to, to counsel their mind and leave them feeling not as alone. I want to be one of the few people in my family to not follow the path of abuse, codependency and addiction. I will be a responsible parent and will never depend on a man for money. I will make my family proud.

ONE KID'S LIE

BY DESTANEE STOCK

"Hey! Aren't you that girl Coy called a prostitute?" this kid on Facebook messages me. I don't even know him; he's just some guy who sent me a friend request that I ignored.

"That was 7th grade!!!" I reply and my body starts to shake. I watch Facebook tell me "person is typing." *Why, after all these years, is someone bringing up such a bad memory for me?* I look at his reply with curiosity.

"So are you still hooking? Can you give me a good price?"

I quickly shut the message box. I click his name and the BLOCK button, and it all comes pouring back to me.

❧

I'm standing in the 7th grade hall of Eagle Middle School. Light blue lockers and mismatched colored tile glimmer under the bad florescent light. I'm wearing black leggings underneath my denim skirt, hoop earrings, and my black and red shirt that reads, "I'm a Vampire (Don't make me bite you)." My brand new white and black Converse shoes are still shiny and my hair is up in a ponytail on the right side of my head with a single pinkish red extension in my ponytail. My friend Kelly and I are talking about how excited I am about my outfit because tonight I'm going to my first metal concert, Mortal Enemy. I'm feeling happy, with a smile as wide as Arkansas, until Coy walks up to me.

I am nervous. My body feels heavy, as if bricks are holding me down. Coy is in my science class and teases me all the time, but I try to ignore him. I don't think he likes that. He's wearing his "wanna be gangsta" outfit: baggy pants and a large white shirt. He has ginger-colored, short messy hair that looks like it doesn't want to cooperate.

I look down on him, roll my eyes in disgust and say, "What do you want, Coy?"

He looks back quickly at his group of friends with a smirk on his face and laughs. "Hey, Destanee, how much?" he asks.

I can't believe what I have just heard. I feel the blood rush out of my head. *Did he just call me a prostitute?* My whole body feels warm in embarrassment.

I gaze at his friends; they're laughing hysterically. Kelly's jaw drops open. Time seems to slow down and my entire body quivers. Tears fill my eyes. How can Coy say something so horrible to someone he barely knows?

I run to the front office as fast as I can. I'm scared but I know I have to tell on him. I can't stop crying. I try to tell the secretary at the front office what just happened, but I can't get the words to come out.

She finally asks, "What do you want to do?"

"I don't want to go home," I say. I am afraid of how weak that will make me look. The office sends me to the detention room to cool down because I can't stop crying. *I know I need the words to come out. I need to tell someone. Nobody should have to feel my pain.*

❧

I'm sitting in the detention room at a plastic desk; I close my eyes, squeezing my knees closer and closer to my chest. I breathe in through my congested nose and slowly exhale through my mouth. As I wipe the tears from my face, small clumps of makeup smear across my cheeks. My face is warm and it feels like the pressure of a thousand fists just hit me all at once; I feel helpless. I'm getting angry just thinking about him. My hand tightens into a fist. *I should have punched him when he opened his mouth. I'm nothing like that.*

I'm ready to talk to someone. I look around the room. The detention teacher stares at me like she might understand.

"Why am I in here when he should be?" I say.

"Who?" she asks.

Then the whole story spills out. It's a relief to have someone listen to what I have to say. My body feels light. I look at her, wiping the last few tears off my cheeks.

In such a sweet mom tone she asks, "Would you like to try to go back to class? I can write you a note for being out for most of the day."

I smile and I tell her, "Thank you so much for everything." I stop at the bathroom before I go back to class. I look at myself in the mirror: my makeup has run all the way down to my chin. I take a paper towel and start scrubbing it off my face. I'm ready to go back to class.

I walk into class and hand my teacher the note from detention. Everyone is staring at me and I feel self-conscious. Some of Coy's friends are giggling. Luckily I see Kelly's worried face so I go and sit next to her. Her sad eyes tell me she's sorry. I answer her with a half-smile and a shrug.

The teacher hands out new assignments. *Everything seems okay. Maybe everything will go back to the way it was,* I think. As I pass by Coy's friends to get my supplies, Hunter Hoffman—the typical skater boy—looks at me with a giant 'I'm going to ruin your day even more' smile on his face.

They are all sharing a Dr. Pepper, passing around the bottle. "Destanee," he says as he taps me on the arm. "Do you want a drink?"

Another in the group says, "Go ahead, suck on my bottle." They all laugh.

Then Hunter says, "Do you spit or swallow?"

I look at him blankly and reply, "What are you talking about?" Before he can say another word I walk away. I stare at Kelly, my eyes wide and about to cry again.

"What does 'spit or swallow' mean?" I ask.

She looks at me in shock and replies, "Is that what they asked you?" I nod. Kelly gives Hunter the worst look she can give a person. Then she explains to me what it means and I run out of the class.

✍

I stare at this guy's Facebook page. *What is everyone's deal? Do people know how hurtful their words are? It has been three years and I'm still a virgin, and they still call me a prostitute.* The BLOCK button is still pressed under my finger. I take it away, knowing that he is blocked forever. I do a double-take of the computer screen, making sure that he is, for a fact, blocked.

My heart pounds. *It's over! I'm taking back my life! I'M DONE!* I feel like I'm in control for once. I log out of Facebook and shut my computer to erase his words from my mind. I take a deep breath of relief and walk out my bedroom door.

✍

I want to close the door on my past—shut it, slam it, leave it behind.
I want to open the door to a new chapter of my life.

✍

A Note from Destanee

After all that has happened, I am finally happy. I don't get pushed around as much and have found some good friends, which I have discovered is key. I know that I have grown from those experiences. Friends leave, lives change, and people grow. Life is hard. Treat people how you want to be treated— it's as simple as that. I am seventeen now, a junior at Scriber Lake High School. I am on track to graduate on time next year and want to become a cosmetologist. To get where I am now was hard, but I did it. I will be getting married to the perfect guy next summer. My family and all my friends are my loves and I hope to be a part of their lives forever. Smiling a real smile is one of my biggest accomplishments. All of the drama, rumors, and harassment are something anyone can overcome. Just remember to always keep your smile!

Thank you for
helping me with my
Story! Love,

Destanee

DON'T CRY, PRINCESS

EMMASARIAH JENSEN

I was kneeling on the crusty red carpet, feeling my heartbeat in the palms of my hands. I knew I shouldn't interrupt him, but I couldn't help the nagging feeling in my stomach.

"Can I have a turn tonight, Daddy? Can I say the prayer?" I asked him hesitantly.

I thought my dad might be happy that I asked to try something new, but instead I got a hindering look and a defeated sigh of exhaustion. The room became quiet and everyone stared at my dad. I looked at him with pleading eyes. We all just waited.

It was Sunday, the day we all kneeled down and said our prayers like we were taught. We gathered around my parents' hard bed, with our hands clasped together and our backs straight. The room was dead silent; the only thing I could hear was my slowly increasing breathing. I didn't exactly know what to do or say. My father was the one with the power in the house. He was a man of the church, so he directed my family.

He turned to look at me. "No," he said. Then he turned away like it was nothing.

I was disappointed and sad. My body tensed and my eyes started to burn. I didn't know what to say next after I had made such a big deal out of it. I don't even know why it was important to me; maybe I just wanted to do something to make my dad happy for once. I slumped my shoulders and focused my eyes on the gross green sheets on the bed, not looking at anybody.

My dad started the prayer. Everyone bowed their heads and closed their eyes, but I felt tears streaming down my cheeks. I didn't think my dad saying 'no' would make me so sad, but it did, and I wanted him to know it. I wanted him to pay attention to me.

"Dear Father in heaven, we thank you for ... " he started.

My family was extremely poor. We lived in an old broken down house where I had to share a space with my older brother and one of my little sisters in a makeshift room that was originally my parents' closet. My two eldest sisters shared their own room and my youngest sister had to sleep with my parents because there was no other place. In total, eight people lived in our rundown, two-bedroom house in the middle of a desert in Utah.

About halfway through the prayer, I couldn't stand it anymore. I stood up, feeling a kink in my knees from being in the kneeling position for too long, and ran to my bedroom. Just before I made it there, I saw my dad raise his head. He shot me a cold, deadly look that made my body freeze and clench. Everything felt like slow motion. I was suddenly petrified.

I frantically looked around my tiny room for a place to hide. I crawled under my bunk bed, bumping into all the stuff that I shoved under there. I started hyperventilating and shaking, trying to push myself as far back into the wall as I could.

I heard shuffling from the other room and I knew he was coming after me. I heard voices, mainly from my mom and dad. They were becoming louder. Dad made sure he was stomping his feet loud enough for me and the rest of the house to hear. I started to feel guilty for making my parents fight, and I knew my little sisters were probably scared. I didn't mean to make this such a problem for my family. I didn't think it would affect them.

I peeked from under the bed and saw my dad's feet. I could hear his grunting and heavy breathing. I knew he was going to hit me. That realization terrified me to the point that I started to say my own silent prayer, hoping that he wouldn't hurt me. He was a huge and muscular guy with a quick temper, but he had always stopped short of physical abuse. I could feel my thumping heartbeat in my throat and ears, and snot started running down my nose.

Now I really had a reason to cry. I felt hopeless and terrified and wished I could rewind time, go back and sit through the prayer like he wanted me to. We all knew how important this was to him because he was extremely religious and practically forced it on all of us. My dad and granny expected us to go to church always, no buts about it.

I heard him coming closer and the only thought that came to my mind was *hide. Hide for your life. He is coming. He is coming to get you.* But I was already pressed against the wall under my bed and had nowhere else to go.

"Emma, get out from under there NOW! I won't take your behavior. What you did was wrong!" he yelled at me from the foot of the bed. "Get out of there, OR ELSE!"

His voice was booming; I could almost feel the house shake from how loud he yelled. I knew he was scaring the living hell out of my siblings, too.

"Daddy, I'm sorry. I won't do it again," I pleaded. I knew it was my fault. I had gotten my family in trouble all because I wanted to have a hissy fit. But I didn't think it would set him off this badly, so badly that he would make the people he cared about scared of him.

I was usually uncomfortable around him, never knowing if I should share my feelings with him because he might think they were stupid and irrelevant. I didn't know if I could ask him simple things.

"EMMA!" he thundered. His voice was so loud and mean.

I tried to push my body farther into the wall, hoping that I could move the wall back and make more room. Tears poured out of my eyes and I couldn't stop shaking. I tried to scream, but my throat wouldn't make a sound. He finally got tired of my charades and laid on the floor so he could glare at me. His eyes looked like what I imagined a mad killer would look like before they took their victim.

He was too big to fit under the bed, but I knew he would get me. My scream finally escaped my throat as he reached out and grabbed my ankle. I looked into his eyes one final time, screaming and pleading "I'm sorry!" over and over again, hoping that he would let me go and look at me like he sometimes looked at me. Like he loved me.

"MOMMY!" I screamed in the direction I assumed she was in, although I hadn't seen her since I ran away from prayer. She had been trying to stop him by yelling at him.

"Shut up and come here," he barked, his voice filled with rage. I thought he might be possessed.

He grabbed my wrist and yanked me so hard it felt like my whole arm was being ripped off. I banged my head on the bed frame as he dragged me out. Then I was finally in his grasp, waiting for the pain I had been trying so hard to avoid.

He turned me over so I was facing the carpet and then hoisted my frame over his lap. I started to struggle, but he just tightened his grip around my waist. I knew if I kept struggling and trying to get away, he would just hurt me more.

My mom was yelling at him to let me go, to stop hurting me, but he didn't listen. I was hiccupping and choking on my own saliva. I couldn't breathe, or move, or even think straight. *Was this really all because I ruined our nightly prayer? Or was there another reason? Was this my fault?* These thoughts ran through my head as I gave up fighting and lay like a rag doll across his lap.

I cried out in pain as the first smack hit me hard on my ass. I didn't feel anything else for a moment and thought he was done. But that was a stupid thought because I felt the sting of his hand hitting me again.. Then another slap on my ass and lower back.

"Daddy, stop!" I pleaded. I hated him more every time he hit me.

After what seemed like fifteen minutes, the beating finally stopped. He let me lay there in my tears and snot before lifting me up. I expected to see his murderous face, but the only face I saw was the face that he usually gave me: a loving one, one that made me feel safe in his arms. Protected.

He held me, telling me sweet coos and sorrys.

"Don't worry, baby, it's okay now. Daddy loves you. Don't cry, princess."

I leaned against his strong chest, numb. I refused to feel the pain all over my body. I couldn't hear my mom or my siblings. I wasn't crying anymore. All I could hear was my dad telling me that he loved me, that he would always protect his baby.

I didn't want to lay there feeling dead in his arms. I wanted to be away from him, I wanted to hate him. I knew if I stayed in his arms any longer I would only forgive him. I knew that no matter what he did I would always forgive him and love him.

I want to close the door to the painful memories that hold me back.
I want to open the door to myself and all the memories to come.

A Note from EmmaSariah

My parents divorced shortly after this incident and my mom moved my family to Washington State to start fresh. At the time, I wasn't sure if that was a good thing or what it would mean for my life in the future. But as time passes by, I can't imagine my life if I had stayed there. My dad and I have lost all contact with each other, but despite his extreme religion and the hard times it caused, I know that he will always love me and I will always love him. This experience has taught me how damaging it can be to force a belief on someone else; it has also made me want to be open and accepting of others and their beliefs. I love the life I have now with my mom, siblings, and my amazing step dad. I'm a freshman and plan on graduating early to begin a degree in psychology. I have many friends and loved ones who make my life happier than I have ever been.

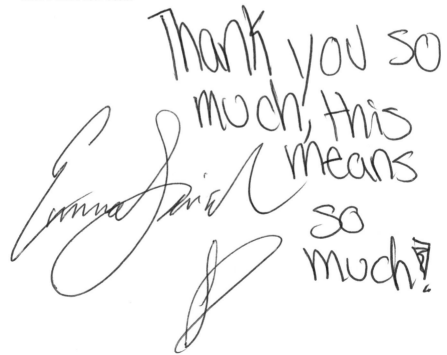

GOOD INTENTIONS, BAD RESULTS

SHELBY ASBURY

"When we walk up those stairs, he's going to be there," the prosecutor says as we make our way toward the courtroom.

Numbness fills my body. I never thought I'd be in court at the age of fourteen.

I take a deep breath. "Let's do it," I say, and start walking. About half way up the stairs I stop dead in my tracks. There he is: the man who took complete control over my life.

❦

A year earlier my friend Jazmen and I were sitting on my couch when my phone vibrated telling me I had a notification from Meetme—a social media website. We had signed up to talk to other teens, just to have fun. I was surprised to see that the notification was from a twenty-five year old man named Jake. "How are you doing?" his message read.

I sat for a minute with my phone in my hand. I knew I shouldn't be responding to somebody so old, but I was curious and felt kind of complimented. We started texting and getting to know each other. We both had similar interests in music and what we wanted to do with our lives. I liked it that he actually seemed interested in me.

When he asked me to hang out in person a few days later, everything told me not to. But I was bored and wanted something fun to do, and he seemed nice.

"Mom, I'm going over to Jazmen's, okay? I'll be home later," I lied, knowing she wouldn't question me because she trusted me.

I felt so cool getting into Jake's 2012 glossy black Camry. His radio was playing "Gunslinger" by Avenged Sevenfold. We went to his house and walked into his bedroom. My eyes immediately locked onto the pistol and the bong on his little table next to his bed. I thought having a pistol sitting next to his bed was cool.

We sat on his memory foam mattress with a green fluffy blanket on top of it. He grabbed his bong and lighter and started smoking. When he offered it to me, I hesitated at first and then I took a hit. I was starting to feel anxiety build up in my stomach because smoking pot made me paranoid.

❦

I spot Jake standing with his family in the hall, waiting to be called into the courtroom. My heart stops and my hands start to shake a little bit. He's wearing a white and blue dress shirt and tan slacks, not a single wrinkle on his clothes. He's a little overweight and limps when he walks. Like his clothes, his red hair is perfectly combed, not single hair out of place. His Marine ring sparkles on his finger, showing that he served for five years. He looks way too calm.

We're all waiting for the judge to speak. I'm sitting on a cold wooden bench holding my mom's hand. Jake is standing next to his lawyer, surrounded by his family. It's quiet and I'm imagining what Jake's family members are thinking about me.

I'm trying to hold it together. My face heats up and I can't control the tears. My stomach is knotting and cramping while my heart breaks into little pieces. *Don't think about that night,* I tell myself. But the tears spill down my face even faster, my eyeliner turning my tears black.

❦

Not long after Jake and I started talking, I felt like he had completely taken over my life. I had never met my dad, so having an older man tell me what to do felt right in a way. But I also didn't like it because he acted like an abusive stepfather; he was rude and put me down. But I couldn't stay away. I got addicted to the abuse because it was the only thing that made me feel something. I had been on anti-depressants for about a year and they made me feel numb.

About a week into our relationship, we were sitting on his bed and he started rubbing my back, his touch sending chills down my spine. "Babe, you should take your jacket off so I can give you a massage," he said. I didn't think this would lead to anything more than just a kiss.

I took my jacket off and then he tried sliding my pants off. That's when I started getting scared. I backed up and he tried pulling me closer, thinking it was a game. My mind froze, but I pushed him away—my bare back hitting the cold wall. He picked up his pistol off the nightstand and put it against my temple. The cold metal made goose bumps pop up on my skin. I looked into his glazed-over blue eyes and saw nothing but hatred. The pistol digging into my head let me know I'd have to do what he told me to do or else he'd kill me. I didn't want to die.

❧

Nine months after Jake and I began having sex, I felt trapped. He had threatened multiple times to kill my family if I didn't have sex with him. I believed he was serious and would follow through, so I did what he said. Meanwhile, I was sinking deeper and deeper into depression.

I had to do something, but I didn't know what. One night I sat on my bed and stared at the pills in my hand. *Is this really worth it?* I wondered. *Would taking these pills really make everything go away?* I felt my heart tearing inside of me, getting more and more painful with every breath. *How I could ever let myself get into a situation this bad?* I sat on my bed in footie pajamas with the arms tied around my belly and a "Yellow Submarine" shirt on. I don't know how long I sat there, but finally I swallowed the tiny white capsules —capsules strong enough to make my body shut down completely. I suddenly felt so alone. I picked up my phone and called my best friend, Madison, who had recently moved to Spokane.

"I don't really know what's going on," I told her, trying not to cry. "But I'm in so much pain, I just want to die. I want it to go all away. I just popped a bunch of pills, I'm ready to leave."

I pictured Madison: her brown and blonde hair, big, brown, beautiful eyes that made her look so much older than she was. She was probably wearing a Sublime t-shirt. Madison and I were complete opposites, but we clicked the first day we hung out.

"Baby," she said to me. "I need you to go tell your mom what you took. I'll be there in a couple weeks. I know stuff has gotten bad, but just fight. I can't lose you." I knew she was trying to hold back tears. When I hung up on her, my body felt a lot lighter than it should have. Knowing how badly Madison needed me, I couldn't do that to her. I walked over to my door, put my hand on the knob and looked at the cuts that covered my wrist. Some were deep; a couple of them were still red and irritated from recent cutting. Seeing the cuts made me regret everything I'd done since I met Jake.

I walked into my mom's room and saw her sitting in her spotless room on her white, fluffy bed. The hardwood floors were cold against my feet as I went to sit next to her. I had always been open with my mom, so it felt terrible to keep something from her for so long—something that was killing me. I knew at least part of the truth needed to come out or I really would die.

"I took a bunch of pills," I said. "Madison is making me tell you, but I honestly don't want to. I just want to die."

I saw intense sadness on her beautiful, freckled face. "We need to go to the hospital, Shelby," she said. Her voice was soft and it sounded like she was on the verge of crying. It hit me how hard it would be for her if I died. On the way to the hospital, I finally told her what I had been hiding for the past nine months. Relief washed over me when she told me she just wanted to help.

❧

A police officer walks into the courtroom and sees me crying. She comes over and rubs my shoulder in a friendly gesture, "We're here for you, not him," she says. Here I was in court with just my mom, while Jake had easily ten family members supporting him—all staring at me with hatred. Her words make me feel like I've done the right thing by coming here.

When the state prosecutor first told me they were pressing charges and asked me if I wanted to go to court, I had said 'no'. I wasn't ready to see him. I didn't go to the first two sentencing dates, either. When my mom told me that this was the last court date, I decided that it was important to go. I needed to show him that I had control of my life.

Even though all of his family is staring at me accusingly, I know I have made the right decision. After feeling depressed and numb for months, being in the courtroom makes me feel alive and in control again.

I think of all the ways that Jake has made my life hell: he turned me into a liar. I lost my relationship with my mom. I became a stoner. I smoked every single day and stopped going to school. I stayed in bed and kept going back to him every time he called. He called me names and cut me down until I cried. I let him say anything he wanted. I actually believed him when he told me I was worthless.

But all of that is over now.

"Do you have anything you want to say before we give you your final sentence?" the judge asks Jake. When he stands to defend himself, all I can do is look at him with pity; I know he will never experience true love.

I block out Jake's words because I know he is just saying whatever he can to save himself. During his speech he looks directly at the judge, not turning or gesturing towards me a single time. As he speaks, I think about all the times he would become furious if I didn't have sex with him. I think about the names he called me or the times he hit me until I finally gave in. Suddenly I feel absolutely worthless all over again. I stare down and watch a black teardrop fall onto the scars on my wrist.

After his finishes talking, the judge calls a recess to read a letter Jake wrote to him. I walk out of the courtroom and sit on a bench, surprised when Jake walks out after me.

He looks right at me. The painful expression on his face tears me apart and I'm not sure how he can still make me believe that he actually misses me. *Why do you look at me that way when you treated me so badly? Is that your idea of love?* I wonder. I turn to my mom and give her a look of despair.

When the recess is over, the judge tells us a little of what is in Jake's letter.

"Apparently, when you were in high school one of your girlfriends raped you and broke your heart, but since that happened you felt the need to turn your pain around and inflict it upon someone else?" the judge asks him.

I can't believe what I'm hearing. A girl raped him? Jake has told me so many lies that I'm convinced he just said that to get sympathy. He's always doing whatever he can to be the center of attention. Why can't he realize that this *is* about him, about something he did wrong?

"Do you or your mother want to say anything before I tell you his sentence?" the judge asks me politely. I shake my head, but my mom walks up to the judge to address him.

"My daughter has tried killing herself three times in the past year," she says, her voice strong. "She has gone to countless therapists and has been taking antidepressants. My daughter used to be a bubbly person, everybody loved being around her. But now she's angry and always sad. If I had found out about Jake, he would have been in your courtroom a lot sooner than he is now."

The judge takes in my mom's statement, and then looks at me before addressing the courtroom. "Because Jake has a mental illness and he is an ex-Marine, we have decided to put him on four years of something called SOSA. He will be registered as a sex offender and will be checked on daily."

I'm so angry I'm shaking. What does Jake being an Ex-Marine have to do with anything? Marines are supposed to protect our country, not tear it apart and rape children. My gut wrenches and I stop listening to what everybody is saying. I blank out and look at the back of Jake's mom's head.

The judge continues, "Because you were strong enough to come here today, Shelby, we are going to incarcerate him for twenty-four hours on top of his four years of SOSA. This courtroom is dismissed."

The judge stands and leaves the room. Jake is put into handcuffs and his family gets up. Every single one of them is shooting me looks of complete hatred. *Why do they hate me? I didn't do anything wrong to them.*

I walk out of the courtroom feeling like I'm the one who just got sentenced to prison.

❧

I want to close the door on depression, a terrible life, and lying.
I want to open the door to honesty and happiness.

A Note from Shelby

After that final day in court, I had some really rough days. Not everything is perfect now, but my days are getting a lot easier. I'm fifteen years old and plan to graduate from high school with an associate's degree, then go on to become a special victim's detective. At some point, I'd also like to open up an automotive shop. Since court, my grades have improved greatly. I have a 3.7 GPA and plan to keep it that way. I'm not the same person I used to be, but I know things will turn out okay. I just want people that are being abused in any way, shape, or form to know that it's so much easier to get help than letting it continue. Although my past interferes with my relationships now, I have an amazing group of friends and I've been dating a great guy for a little over a year now. I hope for nothing but happy days in my future.

LIL RED

TATAM WALKER

I'm standing in the front of Crosby Chapel in Seabeck, Washington, looking down at my favorite person in the whole world, Daunte "Lil Red" Jeffery Peterson. His face is puffy and covered with purple bruises. All of his facial wounds from the accident are covered up by professional make-up.

I'm gripping his cold, limp hand and his ex-girlfriend's warm, trembling one. Or is that mine that's trembling? I can't tell. Standing here staring at him, I want the corners of his mouth to turn up mischievously, like I've seen them do so many times before.

As I stare down at him, I think about the time he tried to show off for the girl that I had brought camping with us. I guess he thought that peeing on the fire would make him look cool.

"Hey! Look what I can do," he had said to us over his shoulder with his sneaky grin. As soon as the urine hit the fire, the embers sparked up faster and hotter, stinging him in the face.

"Tatam, help me! It hurts!" he yelled, jumping up and down. But my friend and I were laughing so hard that we were crying. Daunte ran to his tent with his pants still down, limping, his face red with embarrassment.

But he isn't smiling now. His eyes are closed, like he is sleeping. Ricci tugs at my hand and we go to take a seat on the red pew.

A few minutes later, we all go outside to watch Daunte being rolled out of the chapel to the hearse, and everything is more real because he is leaving forever. Never coming back. Quintin, his little brother, stands next to me, crying.

I hug him and say, "I love you, Q. He's in a better place. He's not going to struggle anymore. He won't get sick."

"Yeah, you're right," he answers. "I love you, too."

Watching Quintin cry crushes me; he's been my "little brother" forever. Our moms have been friends for as long as I can remember, and Daunte and I had known each other before forever. I got his number from the inside of his backpack in preschool, which led to us being "boyfriend and girlfriend." We had been calling each other to talk about everything and nothing—everything except our moms' illnesses—since we were five. We knew that our moms were sick, but we didn't talk to each other about that.

The officiating pastor walks to the front of the church and says, "Daunte will be remembered for his fire red hair and his mischievous spirit. His life touched everyone he knew or met."

Everyone is sniffling. My auntie and Daunte's brothers—Cory, Ryan, Justin and Quintin—are all sitting in the front row, crying. We are all wearing red and black, Red's favorite colors.

I look up from the little folded piece of paper with a picture of his face and the words "In Loving Memory" at the top. His birthday, 04/11/1998, is also listed beside the date he died, 04/04/2013. His funeral is two days after his birthday.

Pictures of Red appear on the screen while "Bless the Broken Road" by Rascal Flatts plays. Pictures of him with his brothers, with our old friend Eric, with his mom's Chihuahuas, and with his mom make me cry harder than I think is possible. My hands are shaking and I can't breathe very well. Still I sit here hoping, wishing, praying that tomorrow I will wake up and this will all just be a bad dream. I still can't believe that I got this news just a week ago.

It had been a normal Saturday morning. So normal. After waking up, I went to join my mom in the living room in my pajamas. As I climbed into my torn-up computer chair, I wondered what was going on with my mom because she was sitting on the couch with a blank, distant look in her eyes.

"What's up, Ma? Are you okay?" I asked nervously.

She looked up at me from her shattered iPhone and said in a very shaky voice, "I'm doing alright, Honey. But your Aunt Sharley, on the other hand, isn't doing too well."

Shit! I thought. I stopped breathing.

"What happened? Is she okay? What's going on?" I said. I was worried because they lived out in the middle of nowhere.

"One of her sons died last night," she answered quickly.

Oh my god, I thought. "Who was it?" I asked, not wanting to know.

While she looked at me with sorrow in her eyes, all I could think was *Please, Please, Please don't say "Daunte."*

But she said, "I'm sorry, baby, but it was Red."

I got up and ran to the bathroom.

After crying as much as my body would let me, I stood up and gripped the sides of the sink. Looking down into the deep dark drain, I tried to calm my scattered nerves, my trembling body and my shaky breathing. I splashed water on my face trying to feel something, and then added a little bit of foundation, trying to hide the puffiness of my eyes. I was trying to look okay for our family breakfast, hoping the makeup helped my white skin tone to look a little less drained. I prayed no one could tell I had been crying, but my raccoon eyes from the liquid eyeliner told a different story.

I hated feeling vulnerable. The cycle of broken promises with my mom and dad were the reason I kept my twenty-foot-high personal brick wall intact. That's why I bottled everything up. Daunte and I had made an agreement that we wouldn't follow in our parents' footsteps, and part of our relationship was keeping each other accountable.

※

The music stops, making me look up. The pictures disappear and Ricci stands up, reminding me where I am and what I am doing. At the front of the chapel my aunt and the boys are standing, getting hugs from everyone, kind of like at a wedding. D's favorite song, "Radioactive," plays all the way home. I guess the saying "Only the good die young" is true after all.

As we pull into our driveway, I feel his presence with me and know that he will always be there. This knowledge calms me somehow as we roll to a complete stop. I slowly slide out of the car, shutting the door with a gentle thud, and enter a world both with and without him.

※

I still want to close the door on painful memories and denial.
I would like to open the door to new beginnings and to my new reality.

A Note from Tatam

The hardest part of dreaming about someone you love is waking up to realize again that the person is gone. It's been a little over year now since Daunte passed away. I still think about him every day. This year will be my last full year at Scriber Lake because next September, I will be a part-time student at Edmonds Community College. I plan to graduate on time with both my high school diploma and my AA in foreign language. I want people to read my story and to know that the strongest people are NOT those who show strength in front of us, but those who win battles we know nothing about.

D, thank you for all your help! ♡ you!

Tatam

COEUR INCONNU

ROGER SILVA

Oh girl
How can I speak with you?
If you could hear my secret
When you saw me
But I couldn't talk ...

—*I want to know* by Hiroyuki Sawano

"Roger." I gasp, inhaling a quick breath I hope wasn't heard until, suddenly, I have those perfect hazel green eyes—her eyes—in my field of vision and looking my way. Those eyes I have known for so long and yet so little and it isn't enough. It will never be enough. I have seen those eyes enough to familiarize her blinking pattern, the number of eyelashes that contradict her eyebrows, and the way her muscles contract around them. I want to lose myself in that safe haven. But I know that's just a daydreamer's dream and most likely always has been.

Either way, it's too late.

"Roger." She says my name again, filling the silent gap between us. Her hair is straight and light brown, running down to her shoulders like a chocolate waterfall. Her attire consists of simple blue jeans, a light blue t-shirt, black converse and a dark brown hairpin.

Dark brown—her favorite color. The one she always uses and runs out of first whenever she draws or paints. Exquisite palm trees, various sorts of foods, fancy clothes and furry animal friends. My eyes used to be on the list of things she drew or painted, but that was a long time ago.

Standing at the center of the bridge overlooking the Agora of Lynnwood High School, surrounded by a sea of students, she smiles to me a sad, knowing smile that I have become accustomed to and I feel my heart clench tight inside my chest.

❧

"This is it," I show her, opening a tattered door that has seen better days. She showed up earlier at my apartment unexpectedly, surprising me with her love and presence. I knew from the moment she knocked on my door that it was the right time to share something with her that I wouldn't with anyone else: my secret spot.

"This?" she questions and I smile at her wandering eyes.

"Yeah, this. I call it the Usual Spot," I say, taking a seat on the all too familiar brown bench in the worn out baseball bunker. On the floor: dirty rocks, used-up cigarettes, and beer bottles lay scattered around us.

"It's messy, I know, but that's because I'm not the only one who knows about this place, sadly."

"I can tell," she says, sitting down next to me. I take off my jacket and place it underneath her so that she can sit more comfortably. Seeing this, she smiles at me appreciatively.

"This was where the old Lynnwood High School used to be before it moved. I found this place and, more importantly, this spot," I explain, gesturing to the bunker and the ancient baseball field right in front of us. "I like it here. It's not entirely private, but it's a really great place to go to when you have a lot on your mind. And, with this view, it's just ... " I look past the baseball field up to the ocean blue sky, " ... beautiful."

"But why show me this? I thought you liked the peace with just yourself."

"Well ... I know, but I was hoping this could be our spot. Just the two of us," I say, willing the blood I feel rushing to my face to calm.

"Our spot?"

"Yeah, our spot," I clarify by holding her hand and giving it a soft squeeze." I was thinking we could meet here every day after school whenever possible and just eat ice cream. The mall is right across the street behind us. And we could go to Cold Stone and order something for takeout, come back here and just pass the time together. Talk about silly stuff and maybe our dreams too. What we want."

She looks away and fixes her gaze to the sky, again, lost in thought. After a moment of unbearable waiting, she says, "Let's pass the time together then."

She kicks off her shoes and stretches out her arms and legs. I expect some sort of complaint, but instead she nestles her head into my shoulder and I hear her breathing relax. "This is nice ... " she whispers dreamily.

"Yeah ... " I reply back equally softly, putting my arm over her shoulder and gently raking her hair with my fingers.

❧

"I'm here," I answer softly and already there's pressure behind my eyes. I blink, trying to come off as if something is in them, and keep my gaze at her shoes. I have so much to say, but none of it will matter.

"It's alright, Roger. No need to look so heartbroken," she tells me, saying my name like everything's normal and she isn't leaving forever. I want to be mad at her, but I still love her too much.

"Right," I croak and cautiously keep my eyes away from hers, knowing I won't find the same amount of devastation in them.

☙

So what do you prefer: chocolate, strawberry, or vanilla?" I ask her while we're taking our time walking, hand in hand, toward the Alderwood Mall. The wind is cold and the sky looks ready to rain, but here with her, I feel warm and safe.

"Probably vanilla. It has the best taste and works well with everything—like milkshakes. And yours, Mr. Roger's Neighborhood?" She laughs and looks at me.

"Oreo," I answer nonchalantly.

"Oreo?"

"Yeah, Oreo," I tell her with a shrug of my shoulders. "It has vanilla in it but the Oreos add a richer experience and, when turned into a milkshake, nothing can compare. It's the bee's knees ... although, it is easy to get thirsty."

"You should join Nabisco then, since you're so passionate about them," she jokingly suggests. I can see where this is going. The banter exchanged between us never seems to end.

"Unfortunately, I can't. But maybe you should. You might need it for your career," I playfully retaliate back.

"Being a tattoo artist is a worthwhile job."

"And becoming a scientist isn't?" I question just as the silhouette of the mall comes into view.

"Who knows?" she ponders softly, looking up at the ash-colored sky. "Time never waits. It all depends on what type of scientist you want to be, Roger."

☙

"There's nothing I can do," she says, trying to defend her reason for leaving and I'm tired of these cliché words. The students around us have unknown faces and blurred quick-paced footsteps. Time is running out.

Suddenly, the last minute warning bell rings and my heart drops dead to my stomach. In a few short agonizing moments, she'll be off to her sixth period class and then on a bus heading home where she'll be sent away forever. These few precious seconds are the last I'll ever have with her.

Hopelessly, I shake my head. I've always had it made with good words but now they have abandoned me entirely.

"Maybe there is." I try to reason with her against fate and time.

But instead she looks at me and says, "There isn't, Roger."

❧

"Come on already!" she says with determination shining in her eyes. She's staring at me, eyebrows furrowed, and I can feel myself already starting to give in.

"But I can't!" I protest weakly, trying to stand my ground.

It's late and we're enjoying the evening at my apartment, sprawled out on my black living room couch with all the lights off watching *Halloween* and eating popcorn. Only now we're both sitting up, Michael Myers is paused, and she's inching closer as I'm scooting away towards the couch arm. I'm trapped. I know what she wants and I'd be more than happy to oblige, but I can't.

"It's okay, Roger," she says, all hints of vexation gone, replaced with sweet sincerity. "I don't mind."

My urge to argue and fight back dissipates just as a fit of coughs makes me hack and wheeze. I turn my head the other way just in time, almost showering her with germs.

"But I'm sick! I can't kiss you when I'm sick because you'll get sick too," I manage to get out through coughs.

"Then take some medicine for once before your cold gets the best of you!" she retorts.

"Never. Medicine is evil. It tastes as bad as the time you cooked ... " I trail off, frightened now and I mentally slap myself for my tongue slip.

"What did you say?" she questions quizzically and my heartbeat speeds up. *'Never insult a woman's cooking'*, my mother once told me.

"I-I don't know," I chuckle nervously. "I'm not thinking straight. You're right, I'll take some medicine."

'When in doubt, kiss her ass.' Another saying my mom once said and I wonder where she gets these bizarre sayings.

I get off the couch and make my way to the bathroom to take the much-needed Tylenol.

Once done, I find my way back to the couch and sit, exhaling in finality. Glancing over, I see she is sitting straight up, some space away from me, watching an un-paused Myers take his first victim in gruesome fashion.

"So, I took the medicine but you could've at least waited for me to return before pressing pla—mmmhhh?!"

My sentence is cut short by her lips suddenly pressing into mine. She ends it with a loud smack of her lips like she had just tasted a fine gourmet dish. The grin on her face, lighting up her eyes, expresses victory.

"Y-y-you just kissed me!" I sputter out after regaining some composure.

"Yeah, and?" The tone in her voice is light and composed—the complete opposite of mine.

"But now you're gonna get sick too!"

"Honey ... ," she trails off and I scoot a little closer. "Who cares? If it's your germs, I don't mind." She smiles as she says this, burying her head into my shoulder and her chuckle reverberates against my chest. I'm scared this feeling inside might be love.

❧

Slowly beginning to sense I cannot change the inevitable, I take a concealing deep breath and say unconvincingly, "Well, have a safe trip."

A small frown appears on her face, finally, and she peers at me almost angrily. "Please don't say things like that, Roger."

"Then don't say things like 'there's nothing I can do' or 'it's alright'. You're *leaving—going away*. You're *okay* with this. Can't you ... can't we just stop acting like this is nothing?" I say, my lips trembling

"Alright," she says, nodding her head in agreement.

"What will you do once you reach your destination?" I ask this question only because I don't know what else to do. I'm imagining impulses of running after her.

"Don't know," she replies absentmindedly. "Search for new stories."

"But there are stories here."

"They aren't the right ones," she says to me in a stern voice.

A knowing look flashes in her eyes and her partly clenched hands reveal that she knows something that I don't. I don't try asking what she really means.

❧

" ... what?" I ask in utter disbelief, my heart skipping several beats in paralyzed shock.

"My dad is sending me away. States away, I mean."

I'm rooted to the ground at the Usual Spot, both of us standing, and a cold fear slowly takes form inside me. I feel sick. I'm scared—more scared than I have been in the longest time. I manage a weak reply.

" ... when?"

"By the end of this week. Friday, Roger." She pauses on my name and I sense something strange in her that wasn't there before: a change. A question, I see, is there in her eyes: *Do you understand?* they ask me.

It's an earnest look, pleading with me to accept this new, profound horror and I don't. I can't. Doesn't she know me by heart now? I can't deal with sudden things like this.

"I-I don't ... why?"

She sighs and takes one step closer. Wrapping her arms around me, she looks back at me and smiles, as usual, but I don't see that light in her eyes. That tender lift at the corner of her mouth just isn't reaching them for all I know.

"I know how you feel but I can't do anything. My dad doesn't want me around anymore. I just found out this morning."

"But what about your friends? Your school? ... Us?" Barely a whisper, the one question I was too afraid to ask left my lips as if it had a will of its own.

"You were the first one I thought of, Roger, but there's nothing I can do."

Desperation hits me. Panic overcomes my senses and overrides my usual calm demeanor.

"My mom said she would adopt you if anything happened." The words come out tumbling, rushing. My brain can't keep up with my mouth.

"That's not how it works," she replies, shaking her head, possibly in exasperation, and I bite my bottom lip.

"I'll go with you then."

Another headshake, and then she wraps her arms more tightly around my dazed body.

॰

Another bell rings and we are late for class, but I can't muster the energy to care about science right now. A flare from the clear blue sky casts downwards, enveloping the area she is standing in, surrounding her in a burst of warm light. She looks like a living angel.

She glances around and it's then I notice from the sudden quietness that we are the only two still remaining on the bridge. Everyone else is where they are supposed to be, diligently doing their work, blissfully unaware of the situation unfolding. I can't help but joke inside from all this. This is something you only see in movies or read about in books: a classic, textbook mushy good-bye scene.

From the bridge here, we're easy prey for autocratic teachers to spot us and send us our separate ways. Sensing this as well, she clears her throat.

"We should get going," she says, sighing so softly I almost miss it.

"Yeah," I reply in stony monotone. She seems caught off guard and I see a small look of surprise in her eyes. She doesn't know it, but it was the way I used to speak to others before I met her. I didn't care about making friends until I met her.

She closes the gap separating us and pulls me in for a hug—her arms soft and warm. She buries her head into my shoulder like she has done so many times before and my heart turns into a battleground. I'm torn between pushing her away and latching onto her so she won't leave—as if she will stay in my arms—as if she's always been mine to have forever.

She lets go of me and takes a step back, clearing her throat against the awkward stifling silence. But as she's stepping backwards, she rushes forward, closing the gap between us again, and seals the space between us with a kiss.

My internal battle transforms into a physiological war and her lips keep pressed against mine: five seconds, ten seconds, fifteen. I'm trying to count the seconds but I can't think straight. The effect she has on me is infinite and unbearable. Her kiss is prolonged like she still cares.

She ends it by stepping away, her eyes cast down. She gives me one fleeting look, long and hard to the point where I almost look away. Softly, but with clarity, she says, "Good-bye, Roger."

Two years of my life begin walking away right before my eyes.

Emilia ...

All the words are there but they remain locked inside. My mouth has gone numb and dry. From the view of the bridge, I can still see her moving away, farther and farther. She keeps on walking, turns a corner, and disappears from my sight completely.

My legs won't function enough to give chase. Instead, they turn and run in the opposite direction, high-tailing it out of the school, running away from the terrifying sense of good-bye and forever.

You're alone in the rain
Been thinking of you
You can't stop your tears
And when you stay with me
Just before
I wanna know ...
Do you love me?

I want to close the door to these awful euphoric memories.
I want to open the door to my heart once more.

A Note from Roger

My heart yearns for something real—something alive. I want to know what's it's like to give my whole heart to someone without them deserting it, leaving it behind forever again. But for now, I'm a senior here at Scriber Lake High School and I'll be graduating this June. When I came to Scriber, I had about four to six credits acquired total. I was told I wouldn't make it, but with perseverance, I worked hard and have achieved a whopping total of nineteen credits. After high school, I aspire to become a firefighter to gain the strength and skills needed to protect the things important to me. I wrote this story for myself to remember.

WHO WE ARE

Back Row: Danielle Goodwin, Emma Norton, Jaycee Schrenk, Tatam Walker, Eli Peterson, Brieaunna Dacruz, Maize Phillips, Robert Jefferys, Jennifer Haupt, Marjie Bowker. **Front Row:** Ingrid Ricks, Roger Silva, Chase Werner, EmmaSariah Jensen, Lilly Anderson, Shelby Asbury, Marika Evenson, Destanee Stock. Not pictured: Brinnon Hall.

Scriber Lake is an alternative high school in the Edmonds School District, located just north of Seattle, Washington. Ours is a school of choice; some students come to Scriber as freshmen, some come seeking a second chance, and some land here for a last chance. The majority of Scriber students have felt lost in the system at some point and many find success in our program. We are a school of small classes and caring teachers who strive toward creative approaches to learning. Scriber is a family.

Though this program is being spearheaded at Scriber Lake, we view the We Are Absolutely Not Okay writing/publishing program as the beginning of a grassroots movement that helps teenagers everywhere claim their power by finding their voice and sharing their stories.

For more information, please visit www.weareabsolutelynotokay.org.

ABOUT OUR PROGRAM

Since November 2011, Scriber Lake High School English Teacher Marjie Bowker and author Ingrid Ricks have been using Ricks' coming-of-age memoir *Hippie Boy: A Girl's Story* as a guide to help students find their voice and power through personal storytelling. This collaboration has so far resulted in three published student story collections: *We Are Absolutely Not Okay, You've Got it All Wrong,* and *Behind Closed Doors: Stories from the Inside Out,* and a life-changing experience for the student authors involved. It's also led to a partnership with Seattle Public Theater, in which student stories were converted to a stage play and performed by other students in a powerful stage performance: *You've Got It All Wrong, Live.* Edmonds Community College recently chose *You've Got it All Wrong* as their Community Read for the 2014-15 school year.

To address the growing demand for this program, Bowker and Ricks recently developed a guide for teaching narrative writing, *Transforming Lives through Personal Storytelling.* This guide adheres to the Common Core State Standards for both narrative writing and reading and includes eight lesson plans for teaching scene structure and narrative content (setting, character, emotion, dialogue and sensory detail). Their student publishing workshop guide will be released August 2014.

To purchase student books or curriculum, please visit our program website: www.WeAreAbsolutelyNotOkay.org

PROGRAM MENTORS

Marjie Bowker

Marjie Bowker has taught English and a little history somewhere in the world for the past seventeen years: in China, Norway and Vietnam, in addition to her "regular" spot at Scriber Lake High School in the Edmonds School District just north of Seattle, Washington. A strong advocate of community/student partnerships, she is constantly fostering relationships with community leaders to help enrich the lives of the teens she works with and was recently recognized as "Teacher of the Year" by the local VFW chapter for her innovative teaching/mentorship style. Past awards include two NEH scholarships to study at Columbia University & Crow Canyon Archaeology Center. Marjie has traveled to more than thirty counties and is always on the lookout for creative ways to infuse her love of travel into her teaching career, including leading two trips to Costa Rica to save the Leatherback sea turtles.

PROGRAM MENTORS

Ingrid Ricks

Ingrid Ricks is an author, speaker, essayist and teen mentor. Her memoirs include The New York Times Best Seller *Hippie Boy* and *Focus*, a memoir about her journey with the blinding eye disease Retinitis Pigmentosa. She is currently working on a memoir about her yearlong quest to save her eyesight, and is blogging about her journey at www.determinedtosee.com.

Ingrid's essays and stories have been featured on Salon and NPR. Along with writing, she is passionate about leveraging narrative writing and the new world of publishing to give teens a voice. Her background includes ten years as a social issues journalist, including two trips to Africa to write about children orphaned by AIDS and war, and twelve years as a PR and marketing consultant with clients ranging from large consumer brands such as Billboard to small start-ups. For more information, visit www.ingridricks.com

ACKNOWLEDGMENTS

This student writing/publishing program would not be possible without the backing of the Edmonds School District and the ongoing encouragement and support of Scriber Lake Principal Kathy Clift. From the beginning, she has understood the power of these voices and the importance of ensuring that they are heard.

We are grateful to the Hazel Miller Foundation for awarding us a grant that funded the publishing workshop and production costs for this book. We are also grateful to the Rotary Club of Edmonds Daybreakers, who have been avid supporters of both our student mentoring/publishing program and Scriber Lake High School as a whole.

Finally, we want to extend a special thank you to Danielle Anthony-Goodwin and Jennifer Haupt, both gifted writers who donated their time, talent and hearts to help students in this year's publishing workshop revise and polish their stories. We also want to thank Carol Bowker and Mary Anthony, who both generously volunteered their time to proofread this book.

CPSIA information can be obtained at www.ICGtesting.com
Printed in the USA
BVOW01s2007180514

353465BV00002B/13/P